Options Trading Simplified

A Guide with basic steps on how to trade options for beginners

Trade Options Team
tradeoptionsteam.com

TABLE OF CONTENTS

Money is exciting because there are ways we can make more of it. But sometimes, trying to get rich quickly makes all our money disappear. Why? Maybe we didn't do it the right way or didn't have a good plan. It's super important to be careful with our money.

Whenever we put money into something, like buying stuff or investing, there's a risk. So, never put all your money into just one thing. Imagine if that one thing goes wrong; you might lose it all. It's better to spread out your money into different things, like various ways of making money or different kinds of stocks. Don't put everything on one bet.

This book talks about a way to make money called "Options Trading." But we don't put all our money into just this one thing. We have some saved up, some in stocks that pay us regularly, and some in the Options Trading ways we discuss in this book.

But what is Options Trading? Options Trading is like making predictions about the future value of things, such as stocks. Instead of buying and owning the stocks, you make contracts that give you the choice to buy or sell them later. It's like betting on whether the price will go up or down.

For example, you might think a certain stock will go up in a month. You can make an "options" contract that says you have the right to buy it at today's price in a month. If the price goes up, you make a profit!

It's a way to make money, but it comes with risks. You need to learn how it works and start slowly. This book will help you understand the basics and some strategies to get started. Remember, it's okay to start small and learn along the way.

But we can't decide how you should use these strategies. Everyone's different. Some people need money soon, like in five years. Others are saving for a faraway retirement in 10 or 20 years. As long as the money we put in grows more, that's great! But sometimes, when we invest in things like stocks or Options Trading, we might lose a bit of money. No one has a way to make money that's always perfect.

The most important thing is to know how much you can afford to lose. It's like having a rule: don't lose more than 2% of your money if something's not going well. Sometimes, if you have a good plan, a small loss won't hurt much. And the other parts that make money might cover that loss. We'll talk more about this in the book.

If you want to learn more about Options Trading, there are lots of resources on the internet and in books. But in this book, we'll keep it simple. We're not trying to scare you – we just want to show that starting with Options Trading isn't too hard. And we will try to avoid all those fancy words that people seem to use when they try to explain Options Trading.

We didn't create these strategies; they're used daily by many others. Our aim is to bring together the ones we find effective in this book, making it simpler for you to choose what might work for you. You can explore more about them through further readings or online videos. But after reading our book, you'll have the knowledge to start trading options. We provide step-by-step explanations of each strategy and how to manage trades that may need adjustments along the way, as well as how to exit the trades if necessary.

In the scenarios discussed in this book, please note that the calculations don't include broker commissions, which may apply to these trades. Since every broker is different, we don't include those fees here. We are using a margin account when we trade, so we will not discuss different types of accounts – just the one we use. Given that readers from various parts of the world may want to use this book and there are different types of accounts and taxes globally, we will stick to the trades we use for our trading.

Make sure to visit our website, tradeoptionsteam.com, and join our newsletter if you want to learn more. Our plan is to share tips and tricks and things we come up with along the way.

But for now, let's get started together. We'll show you some of the strategies we like and use to grow our money.

Welcome to Options Trading – let's learn together!

Important Note: This book serves educational purposes only and isn't financial advice. We want to emphasize: we aren't liable for any losses in your account. Everyone's outcomes differ, and past results might not repeat. Any company mentioned serves as an example. Options trading involves significant risks. Please approach it cautiously and bear this in mind.

Options trading is an exciting and versatile approach to investing, offering traders unique opportunities to profit in various market conditions. Unlike traditional stock trading, options provide the right (but not the obligation) to buy or sell an underlying asset at a predetermined price before or at the expiration date.

Before delving into actual trading strategies, let's discuss the foundational concepts. This discussion aims to make it easier for absolute beginners to understand the upcoming steps, even with the introduction of potentially unfamiliar terminology.

WHAT IS AN OPTION?

An option is a financial instrument that derives its value from an underlying asset, typically stocks. There are two types of options: call options and put options.

Call Option: This gives the holder the right to buy an underlying asset at a specified price (strike price) before or at the expiration date.

Put Option: This gives the holder the right to sell an underlying asset at a specified price (strike price) before or at the expiration date.

KEY COMPONENTS OF AN OPTION

Understanding the components of an option is essential for successful trading.

Underlying Asset: The security (e.g., stock) on which the option is based.

Strike Price: The price at which the underlying asset can be bought or sold.

Expiration Date: The date by which the option must be exercised, or it becomes invalid.

Premium: The price of the option, paid by the buyer to the seller.

ADVANTAGES OF OPTIONS TRADING

Options trading provides several advantages for investors.

Leverage: Options allow traders to control a larger position with a smaller amount of capital, magnifying both potential gains and losses.

Flexibility: Options can be used in various strategies to profit in rising, falling, or stagnant markets, providing more opportunities for strategic trading.

Risk Management: Options can be employed to hedge against potential losses in an existing portfolio, acting as a form of insurance.

Income Generation: Certain options strategies, like covered calls, can be used to generate regular income.

BASIC OPTIONS TRADING STRATEGIES

Before diving into specific strategies, it's crucial to understand some foundational concepts.

BUYING CALL OPTIONS

Objective: Profit from an anticipated increase in the price of the underlying asset.
Risk: Limited to the premium paid for the option.

BUYING PUT OPTIONS

Objective: Profit from an anticipated decrease in the price of the underlying asset.
Risk: Limited to the premium paid for the option.

COVERED CALLS

Objective: Generate income by selling call options on an existing stock position.
Risk: Limited, as the investor already owns the underlying stock.

PROTECTIVE PUTS

Objective: Hedge against potential losses in an existing stock position by buying put options.
Risk: Limited to the premium paid for the put option.

RISKS AND CONSIDERATIONS

While options trading offers numerous advantages, it's essential to be aware of the associated risks.

Limited Lifespan: Options have expiration dates, and their value may diminish rapidly as they approach expiration.

Complexity: Options can be complex, requiring a solid understanding of various strategies and market conditions.

Leverage Risk: While leverage can magnify profits, it also increases the potential for significant losses.

GETTING STARTED WITH OPTIONS TRADING

Education: Before engaging in options trading, it's crucial to educate yourself. Numerous online resources, books, and courses provide comprehensive information for beginners.

Open a Trading Account: Choose a reliable brokerage platform that supports options trading and open an account, preferably one with low fees.

Paper Trading: Consider practicing with a paper trading account to gain experience without risking real money. Some find it beneficial as it eliminates emotional involvement in trading.

Start Small: Begin with a small investment and gradually increase your exposure as you become more comfortable and experienced.

CONCLUSION

Options trading is a dynamic and powerful tool that can enhance your investment portfolio. By understanding the basics, exploring different strategies, and managing risks, you'll be better equipped to navigate the exciting world of options trading. In the following chapters, we will delve into step-by-step guides for implementing various strategies, ensuring you have a comprehensive understanding of options trading.

When you buy and hold stocks, you're likely to make some money, especially if they're the right ones and pay dividends. It's a solid strategy that earns you profits when stocks rise and pays you dividends over time – a steady way to grow your wealth.

But what if there's more? You can start trading options by selling covered calls when you own 100 shares. This adds a new layer of earning potential. Every time you sell an option, you earn a premium. Selling options offers this unique advantage.

Imagine this: alongside your stock's growth and dividend payments, you're also pocketing premiums continuously. Quite an appealing opportunity, right?

With the Wheel Strategy, the first strategy we'll discuss in this book, you can unlock this potential to earn additional income without significantly increasing your risk. It's about adding one more path to increase your financial gains.

Let's dive into the Wheel Strategy and explore how it can enhance your investment journey.

We will explain this strategy, starting with the second part to make it easier to follow.

Let's begin with an example involving a company called XYZ, where you own 100 shares valued at $30 each, totaling $3,000.

SELLING COVERED CALLS

Selling a covered call is like making a deal – you own stocks and offer to sell them later at a fixed price you decide, along with a date. You set the price and the date for this agreement. If the stock price goes up, someone might buy them from you at that price. And here's the exciting part – you get paid upfront for this offer, known as a premium. It's money you keep, regardless of what happens.

You'll check an "Option Chain" at your broker, which shows a list of dates and share prices. We'll choose a date around 30 to 45 days ahead in this list, called the expiration date. Then, we look at a number called "Delta," aiming for around 0.30 or less. This helps us decide which option to choose. And this is where we will find out the Strike Price. It's the price at which we are willing to sell our shares on the picked date.

Let's move on to an actual example instead...

Look at the image below.

Opn Int	Ext	Delta	Bid	Ask	Strike	Bid	Ask	Delta	Ext	Opn Int
						Calls				
17	0.37	0.90	6.30	6.90	28	0.10	0.20	-0.07	0.15	8
25	0.42	0.87	5.40	5.90	29	0.15	0.25	-0.39	0.20	76
114	0.71	0.34	4.30	4.70	30	0.25	0.35	-0.17	0.30	188
36	0.92	0.79	3.50	4.50	31	0.40	0.55	-0.19	0.48	76
14	0.97	0.72	3.10	3.30	32	0.65	0.75	-0.26	0.70	129
26	1.24	0.84	2.40	2.55	33	0.95	1.05	-0.35	1.00	164
98	1.64	0.55	1.80	1.95	34	1.15	1.45	-0.45	1.40	65
87	1.40	0.86	1.35	1.48	35	1.85	2.00	-0.55	1.15	18
29	1.00	0.37	0.95	1.05	36	2.50	2.60	-0.65	0.78	7
24	0.70	0.25	0.65	0.75	37	3.10	3.40	-0.74	0.48	0
50	0.50	0.22	0.45	0.55	38	3.90	4.40	-0.98	0.38	0

In this example, we selected a 32-day date (shown in the middle of the gray line at the top in the image), we look for a delta at 0.30 or less and we find 0.29 in the delta column box. If we follow the horizontal box to the right, we find the strike price of $37. When we sell a covered call at this strike price, someone pays us $0.65 per share (shown as the Bid price), totaling $65 for our 100 shares. This is the premium we get paid for selling this option.

By clicking on the Bid price on the broker's platform, we make the trade. The trade remains open until someone decides to accept it, and we receive the premium upfront.

OUTCOME SCENARIOS

The stock drops from $30 to $28 – If the stock goes to $28 by the expiration date, the other person doesn't buy our stocks, and we keep the premium and stocks. This scenario is often referred to as the options expiring worthless. Then we can do this all over again. We can sell another Covered Call and earn more premium, month after month following the same rules as above. Look for another date and our 0.30 delta.

The stock hits $38 – If it hits $38 on the expiration date, they buy our shares at $37, since this is the price we picked. We make a profit of $7 per share ($7.65 total with the premium) because we once bought them at $30. In total, that's $765 for our 100 shares. The option buyer is happy, since they also made a profit. They bought the shares for $37 when they are now worth $38. But it was a price we were happy with, so we are all happy.

This strategy lets us earn premium income monthly until we're ready to sell our stocks. And if we don't want to sell our stocks yet, we can "Roll" the option to earn more premium and keep them.

ROLL A POSITION

Rolling a position means making changes to an existing agreement you made when selling an option. Imagine it like this: when we sell an option, like we did in the previous example, it's similar to making a deal to sell our stocks at a certain price by a certain date. But sometimes, we might want to change that deal.

So, why do we "roll" a position? Well, it's a bit like updating an agreement to make it better for us. For instance, if the stock price is rising and we still want to keep our stocks, we can adjust the date and/or the price in the agreement. This way, we get to hold onto our stocks a bit longer and possibly earn more money by making this new agreement.

It's essentially tweaking the terms of a deal to suit what we want. In the broker platform we use, there's a simple method to do this by adjusting a few details in the trade agreement. It might differ in other broker platforms. Sometimes, you may need to close a trade and open a new one. You can find more information on "Rolling a position" in your broker's help section or by contacting their support.

In our broker platform, rolling an option is straightforward. You can go to the trade you have open in the position tab, right-click on it, and select Quick Roll to set a new price and a new date. Alternatively, you can choose to roll expirations or roll strikes to roll the price up or down. It's user-friendly.

When you roll a position like this, you're basically moving your initial trade date and/or price forward. Keep in mind, there's a small fee to close the first trade and open the new one. However, this method typically offers a better price, allowing you to potentially earn a bit more. Alternatively, if you prefer, you can just close the trade here and proceed to the next step in this strategy, which we'll cover shortly.

UNDERSTANDING RISKS

The risk in selling covered calls like this is similar to owning regular stocks. It only becomes a risk if the stock falls significantly. So, this is probably one of the best option strategies, especially when compared to solely owning regular stocks.

This covered call strategy using The Wheel can earn you extra cash with manageable risk. Now, let's move on to The Wheel strategy itself, beginning from scratch without owning stocks. Since this is usually how people start. Without any stocks at all.

QUICK INFO: Delta is the expected change in value after a $1 move in the underlying. Delta has a range of -100 to 100 and can be used to express the sensitivity associated with the strike price.

HOW DO WE START?

If you're just starting and don't own any stocks yet, you'll need to get some to start. That's how the Wheel Strategy works. But, as we mentioned earlier, we used an example where someone already had 100 shares in XYZ. Don't worry though – you can also begin by buying 100 shares and following what we showed in the first part. Let's start with an empty portfolio.

Buying stocks this way is akin to what Warren Buffet and Charlie Munger typically did. Both of them, along with many others, don't rush into buying stocks. Instead, they take their time to choose the right moment. It's about entering at a smarter time to potentially make more money compared to buying right away. So, let's guide you on earning extra by purchasing the stocks themselves.

SELLING CASH SECURED PUTS

Now, here's where it gets a bit different. We're going to buy stocks, but we'll use an unusual method – by selling options. Remember when we sold an option earlier? It's a bit like that, but now we're looking to buy stocks using this method.

Here's an example: XYZ stocks are at $40 today. We think the price might drop a bit before it goes up, so we want to buy 100 of those stocks, but at a lower price. We set our target at $38 or lower, 10 days from now.

To do this, we go back to our broker platform's Option Chain – the list with all the dates and prices we checked out before. We search for a date around 10 days away and the price we want, which is $38.

Earlier, we were in the CALL section when we sold our shares. Now, since we don't own any stocks yet, we're in the PUTS section. We find our $38 Strike Price and click on the Bid price to start the process.

Bid	Ask	Strike		Puts	Bid	Ask	Delta
		Calls	10d	Puts			
5.20	5.50	31.5			0.00	0.05	-0.01
4.60	5.00	32			0.00	0.05	-0.02
4.20	4.60	32.5			0.00	0.05	-0.03
3.50	4.20	33			0.00	0.05	-0.04
3.30	3.80	33.5			0.05	0.10	-0.06
2.50	3.10	34			0.05	0.10	-0.09
2.25	2.70	34.5			0.10	0.15	-0.12
1.95	2.10	35			0.15	0.20	-0.17
1.60	1.70	35.5			0.25	0.30	-0.24
1.20	1.30	36			0.35	0.45	-0.33
0.90	1.00	36.5			0.55	0.65	-0.43
0.65	0.75	37			0.80	0.90	-0.54
0.45	0.55	37.5			1.10	1.20	-0.65
0.30	0.40	38			1.40	1.55	-0.74
0.20	0.30	38.5			1.75	1.95	-0.82
0.10	0.20	39			2.15	2.40	-0.88
0.10	0.15	39.5			2.65	3.30	-0.92
0.05	0.10	40			3.10	3.40	-0.94
0.05	0.10	40.5			3.60	4.00	-0.95
0.00	0.75	41			4.10	4.80	-0.95

As shown in the screenshot, the Bid price is $1.40 in this example. This is what the buyer will pay us per share. And since we always talk about 1 option contract, which is 100 shares, we'll get $1.40 × 100 shares = $140 in premium for this trade when we sell this Cash Secured Put.

Instead of buying 100 shares of XYZ for $40 (which is the price today), we're selling an option to someone that we're willing to buy at $38 in 10 days if the price drops below $38, and we also get a premium for this, which we keep, no matter what.

This earns us more money to buy the stocks, which is pretty great, right?

OUTCOME SCENARIOS
The stock drops to exactly $38 – If the stock precisely hits $38 by the expiration date, the other person won't have the obligation to sell us any stocks, and we retain both the premium and our cash. We can repeat this process by selling another Cash Secured Put, following the same rules as before. Simply look for a date and a strike price that you find acceptable.

The stock hits $37 – If the stock falls to $37, the seller will assign the 100 shares to us at the agreed-upon price of $38 each. While the seller makes a profit by selling the shares for $38 when their value is $37, we're content with the price. Additionally, we've gained a premium from this option trade, which we can also subtract from the price we had to pay.

The stock reaches $39 – If the stock rises to $39 by the expiration date, the agreement expires without any action, and it's considered "worthless". The other party keeps their stocks, and we keep the premium, as usual. We can repeat this process until eventually being assigned the stocks at a price we selected, all while earning money while waiting for the right price. It's a strategy everyone should consider, rather than solely buying stocks.

Sometimes, people wait longer to make more money gradually. They might wait for 30 to 45 days, or even 60 days, to secure more cash. You can choose the approach that suits you best.

We utilize both methods – occasionally waiting longer and sometimes around 10 days. This approach works well if we intend to purchase stocks immediately and receive dividends from the company. Additionally, we can sell covered calls, as previously discussed in The Wheel Strategy.

The decision largely depends on whether you prefer obtaining funds without buying the stocks or owning the stocks to earn cash from both premiums and dividends. Of course, this also ties into the hope that the stock value will increase.

ROLLING A POSITION

Like we mentioned before, you can also "Roll" a position with Cash Secured Puts. If the price changes and you want to adjust the expiry date or price, you can roll your position. This involves buying back your existing option for a small fee and selling a new one with different terms. But you can also wait for your option to expire and create another Cash Secured Put, which is something we often do. We want you to know that this is an available option if you need to make changes.

CONSIDERATIONS TO NOTE

Remember these things when Selling Cash Secured Puts. If the company is about to share its earnings or pay dividends before the dates your trade ends, the stock price can change a lot. So, it's safer to avoid trading during those times.

Our broker shows these dates in the Option chain as "E" for earnings and "D" for dividends. It's easy to find if these dates are between when we start and finish our trade.

While some traders work around these dates to aim for specific prices, we play it safe. We avoid making or closing trades during these times for a safer experience.

UNDERSTANDING RISKS

Let's discuss the risks with Cash Secured Puts. It's quite similar to owning regular stocks. If the stock price drops significantly, you might end up buying the stocks at a higher price than their current value. But that's essentially the same risk you face when directly buying stocks.

When you sell Cash Secured Puts, your broker might show a high "max loss" figure. Don't let it worry you! It seems large because it considers the worst-case scenario if the stock price hits zero. Yet, that's an extreme situation rarely seen and is the same risk as when owning stocks directly.

Remember, with a Cash Secured Put, there's a chance you might need to buy the stocks at the strike price you chose if it falls below that. Ensure you pick a strike price you'd consider fair for owning that stock.

When you sell these options, you earn extra money through the premiums until you actually buy the stocks. This way you reduce the overall price you pay when you finally buy them, depending on how many Cash Secured Puts you get to sell before you get assigned the stocks. So, this strategy helps lower the final cost, making it more favorable than buying them directly at the market price. That's why we prefer buying stocks using The Wheel Strategy. And especially stocks that pay dividends. And we always trade stocks that we actually want to own. So there is no problem if we get assigned. We just pay the price we have decided we wanted to pay for the stocks.

TRADING JOURNAL

When you sell Cash Secured Puts or Covered Calls, you earn premiums each time. Keeping a Trading Journal is helpful to track how much you've actually invested and your break-even price. This is crucial because with each option sold, you receive premiums. So, it's not just about the buying or selling price of the stocks; you've earned more money through premiums and possibly received dividends if you owned the stocks on the "x-day".

Maintaining a record of all the money going in and out for each trade is beneficial. You can use spreadsheets like Excel or Google Sheets for this. It's also useful to note why you took a trade and, for some, your mood at the time. By doing this, you can spot patterns in bad trades, understand your decision-making process, and avoid repeating mistakes.

Remember, staying focused when trading options (or any investment) is crucial. Treat your trading like a business, make informed decisions, and never invest money you can't afford to lose.

THE WHEEL STRATEGY – QUICK RECAP

So, let's repeat The Wheel Strategy the way we like to do it. The Wheel Strategy is simple and consists of the following two steps. Just selling puts and calls. Always selling.

SELL CASH SECURED PUTS

Head to the Options Chain and select a future date – choose either 10 days ahead or 30 to 45 days. Next, look for the "PUTS" section and locate the "Bid" column.

Some traders use a -0.30 delta, which means about a 30% chance of being assigned. However, we typically choose a price where we're comfortable buying the stocks if we get assigned.

If we're not assigned at the expiration date, we repeat the process with a new date and price for more premium.

COVERED CALLS

After being assigned and owning 100 shares, we start selling Covered Calls.

Go to the Options Chain and select a date 30 to 45 days ahead. If there is an earnings report scheduled during this time, avoid trading and wait until after this date. Otherwise, search for a 0.30 delta (or less), where the shown price indicates the Strike price for selling our shares at the expiry date.

Click the Bid column in the "CALLS" section, intending to sell our shares at that price.

If the price doesn't exceed our strike price on the expiry date, we repeat this step by selling another covered call for more premium.

If the price rises above our strike price, we sell our stocks and keep the premium. Additionally, if there was a dividend payment during the time we owned the stocks, we also receive the dividend. Plus, the increase in stock price lets us sell the stocks for more than what we initially paid for them.

REPEAT THE PROCESS

Now we go back to Step one and do it all over again. With the same stock or a new stock we like to own.

Since we are going back and doing it all over again, it is like repeating the process over and over again, just like a wheel spinning round and round. That's why they call it The Wheel Strategy.

A better way to buy stocks you like to earn and make money while you wait for the right price.

WHY WE LOVE THE WHEEL STRATEGY

Consistent Income: One of the biggest reasons people love this strategy is the steady income it offers. Selling options generates premiums regularly, adding to your wallet as you wait for the right time to buy or sell stocks.

Lowering Purchase Price: When you sell Cash Secured Puts, you cut down on the total cost of buying stocks. Even if you end up getting the stocks, the premiums you collect decrease the overall amount you spend.

Flexibility and Control: You get to decide the price and date you're comfortable with for buying or selling stocks. This control lets you adjust your strategy according to your preferences and market conditions.

Earning While Waiting: Instead of just sitting on the sidelines, you earn money while you wait for stocks to hit your desired price. It's like getting paid for your patience!

Opportunity for Dividends: Holding stocks can sometimes mean enjoying dividend payouts, increasing your earnings beyond just options premiums.

PROS

Increased Income Potential: You're not just relying on stock price movements; you earn from premiums, dividends, and potential stock sales.

Risk Management: The strategy involves controlled risk, as you choose the price and date for stock transactions.

Profit in Various Market Conditions: Whether the market is up, down, or sideways, you can profit through options premiums.

CONS

Potential Stock Assignment: Getting assigned the stocks. But if you only do this on stocks you actually want to own, then it wouldn't be a problem. Then you can start selling covered calls on this.

Market Volatility: If the stock price moves too fast and a lot, it might affect how much money you make. You might have to buy the stocks at a higher price than the actual market price at expiration.

COMPARED TO BUYING REGULAR STOCKS

Compared to simply buying stocks at market prices, The Wheel Strategy offers:

Lowered Purchase Price: Cash Secured Puts enable you to buy stocks at a lower price, especially when the market drops, reducing the immediate financial burden.

Consistent Income Stream: By selling options, you generate income regularly, enhancing your overall returns, even in fluctuating market conditions.

More Control and Strategy: You have more control over your investments and the ability to strategize around your preferred price points and timelines.

While it's a strong strategy, it's essential to weigh the pros and cons against your investment goals and risk tolerance before diving in. But we prefer The Wheel Strategy better than just buying and selling regular stocks.

So, we now have the Wheel Strategy, which is essentially a more efficient way to buy and sell stocks. However, there are numerous other strategies available. The origins of these various strategies, their names, and configurations are a bit unclear. Some strategies we've encountered, tested, and integrated into our trading toolkit.

One such strategy, sometimes referred to as the "112", is approached by some traders as two distinct trades combined. This method is utilized by traders like Tom King. It's uncertain whether he devised it or if it was introduced by one of his followers. Originally called the "111", it became the "112" upon the addition of another trade to the strategy. We've seen many approaches to this method in webinars and books. But in this book, we'll explain our approach and simply call it "The 112 Strategy A".

In the next chapter, we'll delve into another use of this strategy, referred to as "The 112 Strategy B".

We typically implement this strategy using the /ES (E-mini S&P 500 futures contract). For smaller accounts, the /MES (Micro E-mini futures contract) is more suitable. The ES futures contract has a $50 multiplier, while the MES has a $5 multiplier, making it 1/10th the size of /ES. Our trades typically occur every Wednesday, but feel free to adjust based on your schedule, account size, and risk management preferences.

Risk management will be discussed later in this book.

SETTING IT UP

The 112 Strategy consists of four parts. Start by looking for an expiration date approximately 60 days from now in the Options Chain. While some brokers may limit setting up all four steps at once, we'll review the entire trade, remove two steps, then proceed with the remaining purchase and sale.

For this strategy, focus on the PUTS section. Seek a strike price with a delta around 0.25 to Buy a Long Put Option. Click the Ask column where you see the -0.25 delta to initiate this purchase. Next, select a price 50 points lower to Sell a Put Option for protection, clicking the Bid column to sell. Using these two trades together is referred to as a "Put Debit Spread", which will provide us with a nice little credit in premium.

Finally, find a strike price further away with a -0.05 delta. Click the Bid column to create two contracts, reinforcing your protection. In our broker platform, click the line that appears so it turns gray, allowing you to adjust the quantity to two contracts. Selling two of those puts provides added protection. These are called "Naked Puts".

Confirm the setup and then remove the two -0.05 delta trades. Execute the first two steps using the Good 'Til Canceled (GTC) order option for assured execution. Afterward, proceed to execute the two orders around the 0.05 delta in your broker's platform by adjusting the quantity to two contracts. If your broker allows you to execute all four steps simultaneously, then it's better to do so, of course.

Should you encounter difficulties while setting it up, don't hesitate to ask your broker for guidance; they are there to assist you.

Let's use a real example with pictures to show how we set this up in our broker platform.

We found a date 51 days from now in the Options chain using /MES for the setup, which is okay because we're looking for a date about 60 days from now. We start by choosing the first option to buy at around -0.25 delta. We click the Ask price in the Puts Section, and our broker marks this choice with a green line and "B1" to show we'll buy 1 option contract when we send our order. In this example, the ask price is $37.50, giving us a strike price of 4,670 with a -0.25 delta. /MES was around $4,827 when we took the image.

Bid	A.0	Strike			Bid	Ask	Delta	Ext	Opn Int	Touch	
			Calls	Std	Puts	Last 4,827.25				IVx:14.2% (±160.24)	
222.25	230.50	4630			30.25	31.25			154.18	18	
213.75	232.25	4640			31.75	32.75					
205.50	234.00	4650			33.25	34.25					
197.25	205.75	4660			35.00	35.75					
189.25	197.75	4670			36.75	37.50	-0.25		165.83	14	47%	B 1
185.00	193.50	4675			27.75	38.50					
181.00	189.50	4680			33.50	33.50					

Then, we look for a price 50 points below the first one. That brings us to 4,620 (4,670 - 50 = 4,620). So, we click on the Bid price (which is $29.00 in this example) in the Puts section to sell an option here. Our broker uses a red line and shows "S1" on the far right to indicate that we'll sell 1 option contract here when we send our order.

Bid	A.0	Strike			Bid	Ask	Delta	Lxt	Opn Int	Touch	
			Calls	Std	Puts	Last 4,826.50				IVx:14.2% (±160.49)	
255.75	263.75	4590			25.25	26.25	-0.17	126.75	63	33%	
247.00	255.00	4600			26.50	27.25	-0.18			34%	
238.25	246.50	4610			27.75	28.50	-0.19			36%	
230.75	238.00	4620			29.00	30.00	-0.20	247.00	17	39%	S 1
223.75	231.75	4625			29.75	30.75					
221.00	229.50	4630			30.50	31.25				39%	
212.75	221.25	4640			32.00	32.75				41%	
204.25	212.75	4650			33.50	34.50		170.00			
196.00	204.50	4660			35.25	36.00		176.13			
187.75	196.50	4670			37.00	38.00	-0.25	147.50	14	48%	B 1
183.75	192.50	4675			38.00	38.75	-0.25			44%	
179.75	188.50	4680			39.00	39.75		196.24			
171.75	180.50	4690			40.75	41.75		206.25			

Now, we search for a price with a -0.05 delta. In this example, it's all the way down at 4,300.

Bid	A.0	Strike			Bid	Ask	Delta	Ext	Opn Int	Touch	
			Calls	Std	Puts	Last 4,827.00				IVx:14.2% (±160.20)	
584.00	593.75	4240			6.50	6.90	-0.04				
574.50	584.00	4250			6.70	7.15					
564.75	574.25	4260			7.00	7.25					
555.00	564.50	4270			7.15	7.60		16.48			
550.50	559.75	4275			7.30	7.70		22.00			
545.25	554.75	4280			7.40	7.65					
535.75	545.25	4290			7.65	8.10		25.16			
526.00	535.50	4300			7.90	8.35	-0.05	40.63	2.13k	16%	S 2
516.25	526.00	4310			8.25	8.65		42.16	11		
506.75	516.25	4320			8.50	8.95					
502.25	511.50	4325			8.60	9.10		81.25			

We want two of those, so we adjust the quantity.

In our broker platform, we click on the Bid price ($7.90 in this example), and the same red line appears. Then, we click on that line to adjust the quantity to two contracts. It shows "S2" on this selection, telling us we have 2 contracts on this trade. This is why it's called the "112". These are called "Naked Puts".

Make sure to check how your broker handles these steps, as it might be different.

Now, it's time to check everything. At the bottom left, we see 2 sell options at $4,300, 1 sell option at 4,620, and 1 buy option at 4,670. They all have 51 days until they expire (DTE). We also see that this trade will give us a premium of $8.45 and a max profit of $292.25.

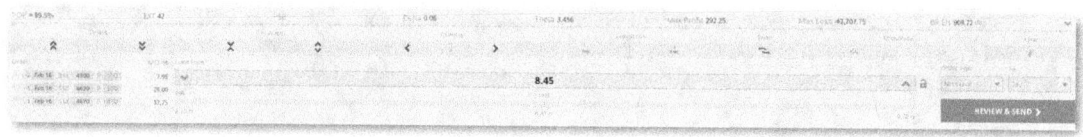

We can now see a curve that shows us our selected trades. Each broker shows this differently, so this image is how it looks in our broker platform.

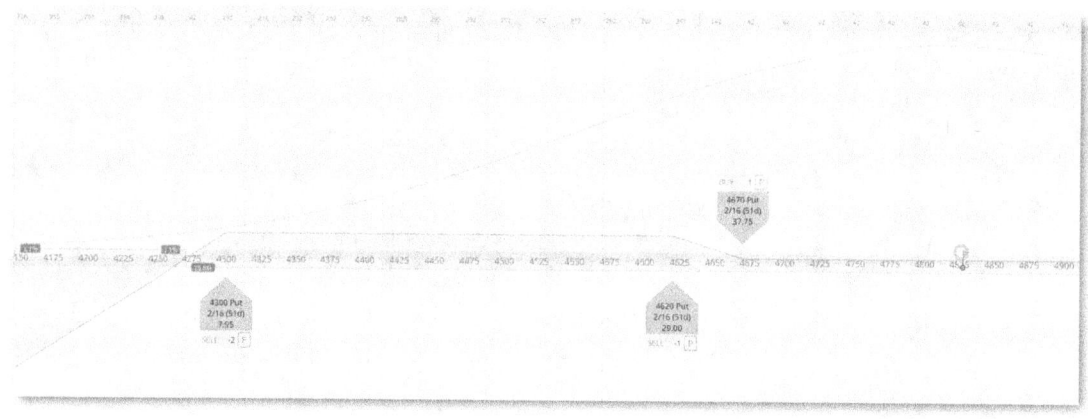

On the right side of the image, there's a circle with a small flag showing where the price is now. On the left side, we have the two trades we chose, which are far from today's price. These are the "Naked Puts". Then, on the right, we have the "Put Debit Spread" we selected, which are 50 points apart.

Looking at the trade outcomes: if the price stays above the two on the right, we'll get $42, shown at the top of the image in very small numbers. If the price drops below the Put Debit Spread, but stays above the two Naked Puts on the left, we'll make $292, which was our max profit. And if the price goes down to the two trades at 4,300, which is rare, we'll need to adjust our position. We'll discuss this further in the chapter.

So, we make a profit if the price stays above the Put Debit Spread or even increases. But we'll make a lot more if the price drops and ends up in the middle of our positions.

While it might seem complicated initially, once you dive into it, the process isn't as daunting as it appears. Since each platform differs, we can only demonstrate the setup based on our specific broker. However, this glimpse will give you an idea of what to expect when you explore this strategy with your own platform. It's all about taking that first step and trying it out yourself to see how manageable it can be.

BUYING POWER

When you engage in this strategy using a margin account which we use, you require what's known as Buying Power. This figure, displayed in your broker account, is crucial before initiating the trade. In our platform, it appears in the section where we review the maximum profit and before hitting 'Review & Send'.

In the image below, you'll notice it shows BP Eff $909 on the right-hand side. This signifies the necessary Buying Power for this trade. However, we recommend having double that amount in cash readily available in your account. That's the benchmark we aim for when implementing trades using this strategy.

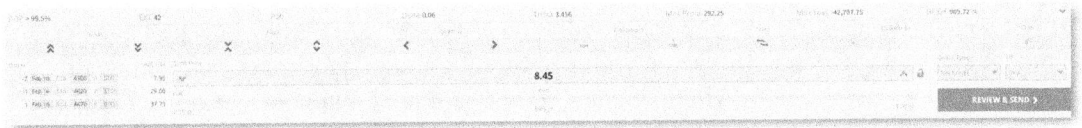

So, approximately $1,800 in cash availability is ideal in this example. If you have more funds and expertise in trading and adjusting this strategy, consider increasing the number of contracts or transitioning to trade /ES, which demands more capital. This means you might make more money, but it also makes the risk higher.

EXIT THE TRADE

Our approach suggests closing the trade at around an 80–90% profit. Then, promptly opening a new position or waiting for a slight market drop to re-enter a trade to potentially maximize returns. Of course, you can opt to hold the position until the expiration date if market conditions are favorable. We might even exit just the two naked puts when they reach 90% and leave the other two until expiration.

Exiting the trade a day or two before expiration is advisable if the market position is between the put spread and the two naked puts. Also, consider exiting if the market surpasses the Put Debit Spread's initial price. If it seems improbable for the price to decline before expiry, closing the position here and initiating a new trade is a wise move.

IF IT GOES AGAINST US

If the price starts going in the wrong direction, we need to make changes to our position. If /MES drops around 3% or more (you can set an alarm for this in your broker platform), or if the naked puts have a delta around -0.02, it's time to check your total profit/loss. If you see a profit, it's a good idea to close the trade. If the alarm doesn't trigger, aim for an 90% profit.

You can also set an alert 100 points above the two naked puts. For example, if we had our two sell options at 4,300, set the alert at 4,400. If it doesn't trigger with one week left in the trade and you're still in the game, consider closing the trade. However, if the alert triggers, you are in a good position, and the debit spread is now profitable. You can sell those buy and sell puts for a profit and then open two new naked puts with around 30 days until expiration (DTE) and a lower delta. Close the two old ones, which may result in a small loss, but you'll receive more premium when opening the new ones, resulting in a small profit.

If you don't mind getting assigned, you can simply get assigned and sell those for more profit. If assigned, you'll own them at a nice discount, and they'll likely go up soon, allowing for good profit. Then you can start selling Covered Calls on those, as we discussed in The Wheel Strategy.

WHEN DO WE TRADE?

If you want to use $10,000 in your account to trade this strategy, then we would say that you should not trade more than 8 contracts on /MES. So, you could probably open a trade the first week in the month (we usually trade this one on a Wednesday) and then another one two weeks after that.

If you keep on doing this, then your trades will expire or if you close them with a profit and open new ones, one after another. This way it will keep running and bring you some nice profit after the first two or three months if everything is going the way it should. But if you don't like to be too active, then you could make one trade every month instead and use twice the amount.

If you have a large account with more than $50,000, then we should trade one /ES contract a month instead. Continue with the same approach, starting with one contract and increasing or adding one after two weeks as you make some profit and your account grows.

Some people trade this every Wednesday and some trade it every Tuesday and Thursday. But we recommend starting slow and learn how the strategy works.

The great thing with this strategy and the way we, and many others trade this, is that it will generate monthly income. Since we put on new trades all the time, it will expire with a profit and the next one will take over and hopefully do the same thing over and over again. And this one seems to work most of the time.

WHAT DO WE TRADE?

If you have a smaller account, we suggest trading the /MES, like we did in the example in this chapter. As your account grows, you can apply the same strategy to /ES.

This strategy also works on Oil (/CL), Gold (/GC), and Copper (/HG). Some people also trade this on Soybeans (/ZS) and Corn (/ZC). Just make sure to check with your broker if there are any requirements to trade these. Usually they require an "Overnight Requirement" when you trade Future Contracts.

The buying power needed for futures options isn't fixed. It changes during the trade. They use something called SPAN margin to figure out how much you need. It's different from how they decide for regular stock options.

SPAN margin looks at your risk and uses 16 different ways to decide how much you need. This dynamic way means sometimes you might need a lot more money than you expected for a trade, even more than what you're risking. If the market drops, then your buying power requirement will increase. So, don't use too much of your capital at once. Let it grow slowly.

When you trade options on the /MES (Micro E-mini S&P 500) futures contract, it's crucial to understand the concept of the multiplier. The multiplier, which is 5 for the /MES, indicates the size of the contract you're trading. For every point movement in the /MES futures contract, the value changes by $5.

So, if you buy or sell an option on the /MES and the underlying futures contract moves up or down by one point, the option's value changes by $5. A ten-point movement results in a $50 change in the option's value (10 points × $5). Understanding the multiplier is essential as it determines the actual dollar amount of gain or loss for each point movement in the futures contract, impacting the options linked to that contract.

For the /ES (E-mini S&P 500) futures contract, the multiplier is 50. This means that for every point movement in the /ES futures contract, the value changes by $50. Similar to trading options on /MES, the multiplier plays a crucial role in determining the dollar amount of gain or loss for each point movement in the /ES futures contract. If the /ES moves up or down by one point, the option's value changes by $50. A ten-point movement results in a $500 change in the option's value (10 points × $50). Understanding this multiplier is essential for calculating potential profits or losses when trading options linked to the /ES futures contract.

When you get assigned and own the underlying asset you're trading, it's usually a great idea to do what we explained in The Wheels Strategy by selling Covered Calls. This way, you earn money on the asset you now own. It works fine with whatever you hold in Option Trading. At least, that's the way we do it, and it works for us.

PICKING A BROKER

As we have some space here, we'd like to share the link to the broker we use. Their platform is specifically designed for Options Trading, making it very user-friendly. We appreciate both the visual appeal and functionality of their platform. With low fees and excellent support, it has been a great choice for us. If you're considering opening an account, we invite you to use our affiliate link, available at **tradeoptionsteam.com/broker**

Strategy 112 B is similar to Strategy 112 A, but here, we extend the Days to Expiration (DTE) to approximately 120 days. Typically, we can close this after about 90 days if it's profitable and then start a new one.

With the longer expiration (DTE), we receive more premium when setting it up. While this provides us with more premium, we should be prepared to wait longer for the trade to expire. Opting for a 120 DTE allows us to reduce the impact of Gamma (one of "The Greeks" mentioned later in the book). Additionally, choosing a date further out in time enables us to use less buying power compared to the 60 DTE we used earlier.

We typically execute this strategy at the end of the first week every month, either on Thursday or Friday, and then initiate another one the following month. As you continue, you'll find yourself managing multiple trades simultaneously. Keep repeating this process over time. For those with smaller accounts, consider starting with one trade each month and gradually adding more contracts or weeks as your account grows.

Considering broker limitations, it's advisable to set up all four legs initially. Use Good 'Til Canceled (GTC) orders for each leg, similar to what we did in the previous strategy.

To begin, search for a put option with a strike price at a -0.25 delta and 120 Days 'Til Expiration (DTE). Click on the Ask price in the Puts section. Identify one put option to sell at a strike price 50 points below the first one (click the Bid here). Then, proceed down to around -0.05 delta and create two more puts.

> If you encounter multiple options with a -0.05 delta, consider choosing the one with the highest open interest. Higher open interest suggests more active trading, making it easier to buy or sell your options. Check your broker platform to see if this information is available, as it can be a valuable factor in your decision-making process.

The only difference is the Days to Expiration (DTE), which is 60 in 112 A, and here we use 120 DTE instead. This strategy is applicable to /ES or /MES, depending on the account size. For /ES, an account size of at least $50,000 is recommended. Otherwise, we suggest trading the /MES until then.

POSSIBLE MODIFICATIONS

In case the market moves unfavorably, you can implement the same adjustments discussed in the previous chapter, following the same strategy. Alternatively, consider rolling the two short options to a farther expiration date to manage risk. Another option is to purchase two more out-of-the-money put options to limit potential losses. However, we prefer the adjustments discussed before. We mention these alternatives so that you are aware there are several ways to adjust if needed.

WHEN TO EXIT
If you opt for a stop loss, it's advisable to exit the trade when the loss equals the maximum profit for that specific trade. Alternatively, you can allow the trade to expire and consider accepting assignment at a favorable discount, which aligns with our preferred approach.

SETTING IT UP
Let's walk through a real example with images to illustrate how we set up this strategy in our broker platform.

Firstly, we found a date 114 days from now in the Options chain using /MES for the setup, as we typically look for a date around 120 days from now. Choosing the first option to buy at around -0.25. Clicking the Ask price in the Puts Section, our broker marks this choice with a green line and "B1" to indicate we'll buy 1 option contract when we send our order. In this example, the ask price is $65.75, resulting in a strike price of 4,950 with a -0.25 delta. The screenshot was taken when /MES was around $5,189.

○ Delta	Bid	Ask	▲ Strike		Bid	Ask	○ Delta	○ Ext	○ Opn Int	○ Touch %
			Calls	114d	Puts	Last 5,189.00				IVx: 14.9% (±264.98)
0.69	660.50	667.00	4550		23.50	24.00	0.09	113.15	54	12%
0.34	613.75	621.00	4600		26.00	26.75	-0.10	131.85	49	20%
0.87	568.25	574.50	4650		29.25	29.75	-0.11	149.50	101	15%
0.85	522.25	529.25	4700		31.25	35.00	0.13	165.64	116	25%
0.94	477.75	484.25	4750		35.50	39.25	0.15	186.64	267	29%
0.82	433.50	440.00	4800		40.50	44.25	0.17	211.80	254	33%
0.73	6.00	397.00	4850		46.25	50.25	-0.19	241.51	283	37%
0.77	348.25	354.75	4900		53.50	57.25	-0.22	276.57	193	43%
0.73	124.00	313.75	4950		63.50	65.75	-0.25	321.85	206	50% B 1
0.70	268.50	275.00	5000		71.50	75.75	0.29	373.26	36	57%
0.68	72.00	237.00	5050		85.50	88.00	0.33	431.97	3	66%
0.64	52.00	202.25	5100		98.00	102.25	0.43	500.95	5	72%
0.56	165.50	169.75	5150		115.00	119.50	0.42	559.82	2	82%
0.51	136.50	141.00	5200		137.00	139.50	0.48	645.40	1	26%
0.45	111.00	115.25	5250		158.75	163.00	0.53	500.72	3	89%
0.33	86.75	93.00	5300		185.50	190.00	0.59	384.50	0	69%

Next, we look for a price 50 points below the first one, leading us to 4,900 (4,950 - 50 = 4,900). Clicking on the Bid price ($53.50 in this example) in the Puts section, our broker uses a red line and shows "S1" on the far right to indicate that we'll sell 1 option contract here when we send our order.

☼ Delta	Bid	Ask	▲ Strike		Puts	Bid	Ask	☼ Delta	☼ Ext	☼ Opn Int	☼ Touch %	
			Calls	1140		Last	5,189.00				IVx: 14.9% (±264.98)	
0.89	659.75	666.00	4550			23.50	24.00	-0.09	118.75	54	18%	
0.88	612.75	619.75	4600			26.25	26.75	0.10	131.88	49	20%	
0.87	567.25	573.50	4650			29.25	29.75	-0.11	147.50	102	23%	
0.85	521.25	528.25	4700			31.25	35.25	0.13	165.68	116	25%	
0.84	476.50	483.25	4750			35.50	39.50	0.15	186.64	257	29%	
0.82	432.50	439.00	4800			40.50	44.50	-0.17	211.80	254	33%	
0.79	389.25	396.00	4850			46.50	50.25	0.19	241.59	203	37%	
0.77	347.25	353.75	4900			53.50	57.50	-0.22	276.37	193	43%	S 1
0.73	307.00	313.00	4950			63.75	66.00	0.25	321.65	206	50%	B 1
0.70	267.50	274.00	5000			73.75	76.25	0.29	372.26	35	57%	
0.66	231.50	236.25	5050			85.75	88.25	0.33	431.07	3	66%	
0.61	196.75	201.25	5100			98.50	102.75	0.37	500.95	5	77%	
0.56	165.00	169.25	5150			115.50	119.75	0.42	585.02	2	89%	
0.51	136.00	140.25	5200			137.50	140.00	0.48	635.40	3	98%	
0.45	110.50	114.75	5250			159.25	163.50	0.53	500.72	3	89%	
0.39	88.25	92.50	5300			186.00	190.75	0.59	384.56	0	80%	

Now, we search for a price with a -0.05 delta. In this example, it's at 4,250. To get two of those, we adjust the quantity. In our broker platform, clicking on the Bid price ($13.25 in this example) shows the same red line. If we click that line again, making it grey, we can adjust the quantity to two contracts, displayed as "S2".

Make sure to check how your broker handles these steps, as procedures may vary.

☼ Delta	Bid	Ask	▲ Strike		Puts	Bid	Ask	☼ Delta	☼ Ext	☼ Opn Int	☼ Touch %	
			Calls	1140		Last	5,189.00				IVx: 14.9% (±264.98)	
0.96	1,330.75	1,337.25	3850			7.25	7.45	-0.02	36.75	20	5%	
0.96	1,282.25	1,288.75	3900			7.80	7.95	-0.02	39.33	27	6%	
0.96	1,233.75	1,240.25	3950			8.35	8.55	-0.03	42.25	50	6%	
0.95	1,185.25	1,191.75	4000			9.00	9.20	-0.03	45.50	137	7%	
0.95	1,136.75	1,143.25	4050			9.70	9.90	-0.03	49.00	148	7%	
0.95	1,088.50	1,094.75	4100			10.25	10.75	0.04	52.50	320	8%	
0.94	1,040.25	1,046.50	4150			11.25	11.75	0.04	57.50	450	8%	
0.94	992.00	998.50	4200			12.25	12.50	0.04	61.88	173	9%	
0.94	944.00	950.25	4250			13.25	13.75	-0.05	67.50	286	10%	S 2
0.93	896.00	902.50	4300			14.50	15.00	-0.05	73.75	236	11%	
0.93	848.25	854.75	4350			15.75	16.00	-0.06	79.38	71	12%	
0.92	800.75	807.00	4400			17.25	18.00	0.06	88.13	187	13%	
0.91	753.25	759.75	4450			19.25	19.75	0.07	97.50	29	14%	
0.90	705.75	713.00	4500			21.25	21.75	-0.08	107.50	62	16%	

Now, it's time to review everything. At the bottom left, we see 2 sell options (marked with a minus indicating it's a sell) at $4,250, 1 sell option (marked with a minus as well) at 4,900, and 1 buy option at 4,950. They all have 114 days until they expire (DTE). This trade will yield a premium of $18.00, with a max profit in this example of $340. This profit is realized if the price moves down between our spreads and naked puts.

Bracket		Strikes		Width		Quantity	
{}	☆	☆	☆	☆	☆	‹	›
Order		/MESU4	Limit Price				
-2 Jun 21 114d 4250 P STO		13.25	✔				**18.00**
-1 Jun 21 114d 4900 P STO		54.00	nat				theo mid
1 Jun 21 114d 4950 P BTO		66.25					
			14.25 cr				18.00 cr

The image below shows the curve representing our selected trades, each broker displays this differently. On the right side, a circle with a small flag indicates the current price ($5,084 right now). On the left, we have the two trades we chose, which are far from today's price (the "Naked Puts"). On the right, we have the "Put Debit Spread" we selected, spaced 50 points apart (4,900 and 4,950).

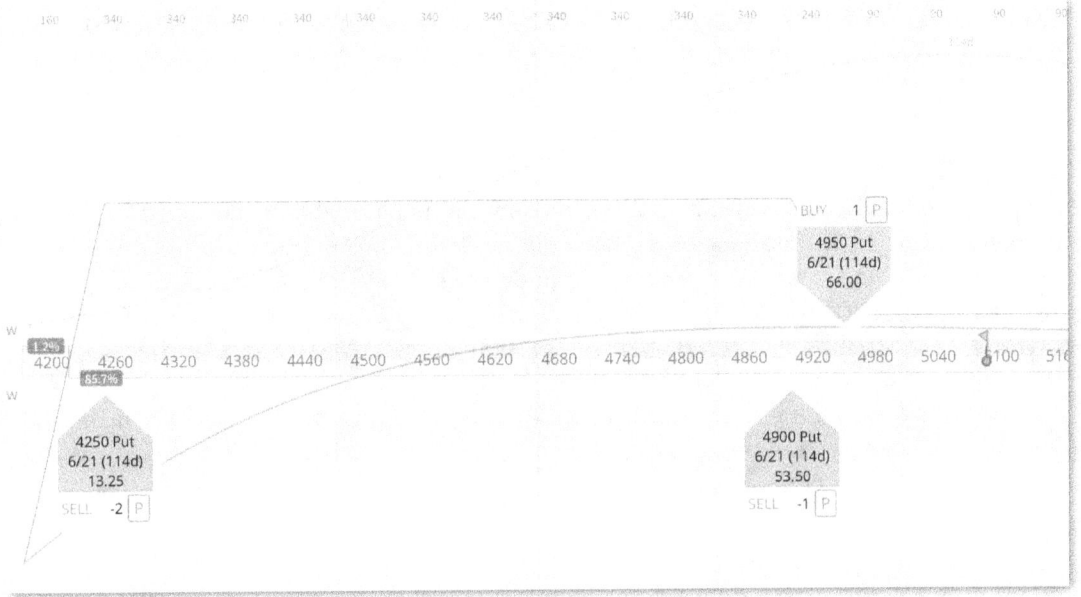

Considering trade outcomes: If the price stays above the two on the right, we'll get $90. If it drops below the Put Debit Spread but stays above the two Naked Puts on the left, we'll make $340, which is our maximum profit. If the price goes down to the two trades at 4,250, which is rare, we'll need to adjust our position or be assigned.

The lower horizontal line displayed in the above image represents Theta. Think of Theta as a clock ticking in the background while you're trading. It indicates how much the value of your option might change over time. Since this value fluctuates, the Theta line will also move as we approach the expiry date.

Now, when you're using a strategy, like the one we're discussing, the amount of profit you can make depends on how fast or slow this clock (Theta) is ticking. In the beginning, the clock ticks more slowly, and as time goes on, it starts ticking a bit faster.

If the markets would drop really quick in the beginning of the trade, the profit between our puts would not be as high as shown. That Theta line will slowly move upwards as time goes.

So, if you want to make the most profit, you aim to close your trade when the clock is ticking slowly. That's when you get the best value for the option you're trading. As time passes, and the clock ticks faster, the potential profit may not be as high. In simple terms, it's like selling something at its best price before its value changes too much over time. That's why keeping an eye on Theta is important in this kind of trading strategy.

In essence, we make a profit if the price stays above the Put Debit Spread or even increases. However, we'll make significantly more if the price drops and ends up in the middle of our positions.

Though it may appear complex at first glance, delving into the process reveals that it's not as intimidating as it seems. Keep in mind that each trading platform is unique, and we can only showcase the setup using our specific broker. Nevertheless, this insight provides a glimpse into what you might encounter when implementing this strategy on your own platform. Taking that initial step and experiencing it firsthand will show you how manageable and rewarding the process can be.

EXIT THE TRADE

We prefer closing the trade when it reaches approximately an 80% profit. Following this, you have the option to open a new position or wait for a minor market downturn to re-enter, potentially maximizing returns. Alternatively, holding the position until the expiration date is viable under favorable market conditions.

It's advisable to exit the trade a day or two before expiration, especially if the market position is between the put spread and the two naked puts. Another consideration is to exit if the market surpasses the initial price of the Put Debit Spread. If the likelihood of a price decline before expiry seems low, closing the position at this point and initiating a new trade is a prudent decision.

IF IT GOES AGAINST US

Should the market take an unfavorable turn, adjustments to our position become imperative. Keep an eye on /MES – if it experiences a drop of approximately 3% or more (consider setting an alarm for this in your broker platform), or if the naked puts display a delta around -0.02, it signals a check on your overall profit/loss. Closing the trade is prudent if you're in profit. In cases where the alarm doesn't trigger, the target remains an 80% profit.

Another alert can be set, this time positioned 100 points above the two naked puts. For instance, if your two sell options are at 3,900, set the alert at 4,000. If, with one week left in the trade, the alert remains untouched, contemplate closing the trade. However, if the alert activates, you find yourself in a favorable position, and the debit spread is now profitable. Capitalize on this by selling both the buy and sell puts for a profit. Subsequently, open two new naked puts with approximately 30 days until expiration (DTE) and a lower delta. Closing the two old positions might incur a small loss, but the new ones will give you a higher premium, ultimately resulting in a small profit.

For those comfortable with the prospect of assignment, getting assigned and selling for additional profit is an option. Getting these at a favorable discount provides an opportunity for potential future gains. This can pave the way for implementing Covered Calls, a strategy we discussed in-depth in The Wheel Strategy.

Now, let's explore a strategy known as Strangles. The way it's set up here is somewhat "safer" than how many others approach this type of strategy. This is a setup we've learned from Tom King and other traders. The strategy boasts a pretty good win rate, and we prefer using it with a 90-day time frame to maximize premium potential.

WHAT IS A STRANGLE?

When executing a strangle, we sell a put option and simultaneously sell a call option. These options are positioned far away from each other and the same expiration date, with the price residing between them. This strategy is used when a trader expects a significant price movement in the underlying asset but is uncertain about the direction (up or down). Our goal is for the price to stay within this range until we decide to close our trade, typically when we've made a 50% profit on the premium.

Traders use a strangle for a few key reasons.

Volatility Expectation: A strangle is employed when the trader anticipates a significant price movement in the underlying asset. It doesn't matter if the price goes up or down; the goal is to profit from the volatility.

Flexibility: Unlike some strategies that require predicting the specific direction of the price movement, a strangle allows traders to be more flexible. As long as there is a substantial move, the strategy can be profitable.

Maximizing Premium Potential: By selling both a call and a put option, the trader collects premiums (fees) for both. This can enhance the potential profit if the price moves as anticipated.

We prefer trading /ES for this strategy (/MES for smaller accounts), but it can also be applied to Oil, Gold, Copper, and several other futures. A golden rule is not to use more than 2% of your net liquidity, a good practice in all scenarios.

To start, we select a date close to 90 days to expiration (DTE). On the PUT side, we look for a delta around -0.07 and click on the Bid price. Moving to the CALL side, we aim for a delta around 0.06, slightly lower than what we targeted on the put side. We then click on the Bid price for this part of the trade. Now, we have a sell order on each side, creating what is referred to as a Strangle. We use different deltas during setup to create a "skew".

> What is a skew? Traders often use a skew, to their advantage. For example, in a strategy like a strangle, the skew allows you to collect more premium for the options that are further away from the current stock price. This increased premium can provide a larger buffer or potential profit in the trade.

You can certainly use different values, like -0.05 and 0.04 delta, to make it even wider. The choice is yours, and the wider you place them, the higher the probability of being profitable. Some traders prefer placing them closer to the price, even with a relatively high delta value, but that's not our approach.

When seeking a good trading opportunity with this strategy, we like to use technical indicators to see the price range. Many free charts are available online, such as TradingView and Yahoo Finance. We use the one in our broker platform, where we look at the Weekly chart, adding the 3ATR indicator with standard settings.

We aim for the price on the chart to be around the middle of this indicator for this strategy. We avoid to trade when the price is too close to the upper or lower bands; instead, we want it somewhere in the middle of the range. When you've determined the levels for your trade with the chosen delta, you can look at these numbers on the chart, showcasing where the price needs to stay within during the trade. Typically, these levels end up being outside the lines indicated by the 3ATR indicator, which is what we prefer.

While we won't dive deep into chart analysis in this book, we want you to know that it's possible to use charts when executing a trade like this. You don't have to use charts at all if you don't like, but now you know it's an option. Using just the delta values, as we do, can work fine as well, at least the way we prefer to trade Strangles.

IF IT GOES AGAINST US

Setting a Stop Loss is a crucial risk management step. We recommend placing it at 3× the premium received. However, keep in mind that, since you've already collected one premium, the effective Stop Loss becomes only 2 times that amount. This safety net provides a buffer in case the trade doesn't go as planned.

If the price starts moving unfavorably, it's essential to adjust the trade. Specifically, if the price reaches around 0.3 delta, consider rolling the option on the opposite side, which is now farther away from the price. Roll this position just outside the expected move, typically indicated in your broker platform's Option Chain.

Using the alarm function in your broker account is a great way to set up these levels. Place an alarm where the price indicates an adverse movement and another for the Stop Loss. Alternatively, you can set up a Stop Loss in your broker account, although the process may vary. In our broker, we right-click on the order, select "Close Order," adjust the price for the Stop Loss, and set it as GTC (Good 'til cancelled).

It's crucial to note that the price you set is for when the market is open. If something unexpected happens overnight and the price drops further, your market order will execute at that price, not the one you set.

Consider changing your Take Profit target to 25%. Making a smaller profit is a prudent move if the trade goes against you. In some instances, it might be wise to close the trade if no profit is made when there are 21 days left until expiration, mitigating potential losses.

These adjustments aim to safeguard your investment and provide flexibility in response to market movements. Remember, managing risks is a key element of successful trading.

Standard deviation in options trading is like a tool that measures how much the price of something, like the Micro E-mini S&P 500, usually changes. It helps us guess how much the price might go up or down in the future by looking at how much it moved in the past. This way, we can try to figure out how risky or safe a trade might be and make smarter decisions.

Now it's time for The Monday Strategy, a simple yet powerful approach to trading on the /MES (Micro E-mini S&P 500) or the /ES (E-mini S&P 500) futures market (depending on your account size). We'll walk through the key components of the strategy, providing step-by-step guidance on execution, optimal timeframes, and profit targets. But before we dive into the details, let's explore the rationale behind this strategy and understand how it fits into the dynamic world of futures trading.

The Strategy is a testament to the idea that strategic, well-calculated moves can yield consistent returns. By leveraging the unique characteristics of the /MES market, this strategy offers traders an opportunity to generate a steady income with a structured and disciplined approach. So, whether you're just starting your trading journey or looking to enhance your existing strategies, let's unravel the intricacies of The Monday Strategy and empower you to navigate the futures market with confidence and success.

This strategy involves trading on /MES. The goal is to sell a naked put with a very low delta, usually around -0.05 to -0.10. To execute this, navigate to the PUT side and place a Sell option by clicking on the Bid price.

We prefer a 60-day expiration date (DTE) for this strategy and aim for an 80% profit. Keep in mind that /MES has a 5× premium multiplier, impacting the commission you pay. Commission fees can vary among brokers and might not be directly tied to the multiplier. They're usually charged per contract or per trade, varying based on the broker's fee schedule. Review your broker's commission structure to understand how fees are calculated for futures contracts or options.

Our target is to achieve an 80% profit, automated in our broker platform, usually within 30 days. It's crucial to maintain the same buying power displayed in cash in your account during the trade. For instance, if the buying power shows $300, ensure you have $300 available in cash. If you're more conservative, consider setting aside around $1,000 per trade since buying power fluctuates during these trades.

For example, if you plan to execute one trade weekly, you'll need $4,000 available cash in your account for one month. If you plan to trade five contracts, a little over $20,000 will be necessary. Start with one contract per week, then gradually increase the quantity based on your account size and available cash.

Upon trade closure, immediately initiate a new one to maintain a continuous flow of trades. This consistent approach usually yields around a 2% profit per month, a respectable return.

IF IT GOES AGAINST US
Setting an alert at approximately 0.3 delta when initiating the trade is wise. If the alert triggers, it's time to roll the trade. Buy back the current one and open a new position, extending the expiration by a month, aiming for the same premium. This can usually be easily done in one go on most broker platforms. Right-click the trade and roll in date and price.

This maneuver might not yield a profit; it could break even. However, it's a way to exit a trade that doesn't align with our expectations. If the market experiences a slight downturn, consider adding one more trade if you have available cash. Doubling the trades could lead to a better chance of ending with a favorable profit, instead of the one that didn't work out for us.

SETTING IT UP

The Monday Strategy is a great one to use on /MES and this is what it looks like in our broker platform.

We go to the Options Chain and select a date around 60 days from now. In the image below we found one 61 days from now, which is good enough. In the top grey line you see 61d, which indicates the DTE.

Open Int	Ext	Delta	Bid	Ask	Strike		Bid	Ask	Delta	Ext	Open Int
Mar 15, 2024 /MESH4 (MES) AM					Calls / 61d / Puts						IV: 14.3% (±174.82)
16.87	5.93		785.25	792.50	4025		1.50	6.40	-0.03	78.33	24
17.25	0.98		760.75	768.25	4050		2.25	6.30	0.03	30.65	4.75K
18.69	0.98		736.00	743.50	4075		2.90	7.15		31.77	
25.11	0.97		711.50	766.00	4100		5.10	6.95		33.85	1.57K
23.29	0.97		691.75	699.00	4120		5.80	7.40		32.??	
21.66	0.97		686.00	693.00	4125		5.50	7.50		35.31	
21.93	0.97		681.75	689.25	4130		7.00	7.60		38.25	0
22.90	0.97		672.00	679.50	4140		7.15	7.75		37.??	
18.97	0.97		662.25	669.50	4150		6.25	7.95		38.??	4.93K
25.97	0.97		652.25	659.75	4160		7.55	8.15		39.2?	
26.16	0.97		642.75	650.00	4170		7.75	8.35		40.2?	
28.71	0.97		638.00	645.25	4175		6.15	8.45		40.75	19?
27.26	0.96		633.00	640.25	4180		7.95	8.60		41.25	
28.36	0.96		623.00	630.50	4190		8.15	8.80		42.30	
29.32	0.96		614.75	619.50	4200		7.35	9.05	0.05	43.50	349	51
	0.96		603.75	611.00	4210		8.65	0.30		44.??	
	0.96		593.75	601.25	4220		8.90	0.55		45.95	

Then we looked for a delta around -0.05 and -0.10 and we found several at -0.05, but we picked the one with a higher open interest (349 shown in the image). Then we clicked on the Bid price for the 4,200 Strike price. This will give us a premium of $7.35 which is $36.75 with the 5×multiplier for /MES.

We select GTC (Good 'Til Cancelled) and click on Review and Send to check that everything looks correct. And then we enter the trade.

When the trade is filled, we move up to our positions tab and right click on this trade and look to close with a 80% profit. We click the up arrow until it shows 80 and put on that trade, which will then show up in our account as a trade waiting to be triggered. As soon as it reaches a 80% profit on our premium, which in this example will be $29.40. Usually we reach this within 30 days.

We also like to put on an alarm in our broker platform. We look for a price where the price is moving closer to our strike price. In this example /MES is around 4,811 and we placed our strike price at 4,200. We would probably set the alarm around 4,400.

You can read how to set an alarm in the chapter called Alerts in this book.

And if you put on a trade like this every Monday, you will also grow your account slowly. And if your account size is large enough, you can increase the number of contracts for each trade. If you use 2 contracts you would of course make the double in collected premium – if everything is going our way every time.

But, like we discussed earlier, if the market is moving against us, we can always roll a position a month ahead and maybe lower our take profit as well.

Embarking on the journey of trading iron condors opens the door to a nuanced yet powerful strategy in the options trading realm. Ideal for navigating neutral market landscapes, the iron condor offers income-generation potential with built-in risk management. Let's delve into the intricate details, focusing on how to strategically structure an iron condor and manage associated risks.

UNDERSTANDING THE IRON CONDOR LEGS

The essence of an iron condor lies in the careful orchestration of four options, forming two credit spreads. On the call side, an out-of-the-money (OTM) call is sold, and a further OTM call is bought to limit potential losses – this constitutes the bear call spread. Simultaneously, on the put side, an OTM put is sold, and a further OTM put is purchased to construct the bull put spread. This multi-leg strategy seeks to capitalize on low volatility and sideways market movement.

SELECTING STRIKES AND PREMIUM COLLECTION

Choosing the right strike prices is important. Traders typically look for a wide profit zone, achieved by selling options with strike prices further away from the current market price. This strategic placement contributes to premium collection, a key aspect of the iron condor's income-generation capability. Employing delta as a guide can aid in selecting strikes. We usually look for a delta around -0.16 on the put side and 0.16 on the call side when we sell the first ones.

RISK MANAGEMENT AND CALCULATING MAXIMUM LOSS

While the iron condor presents an opportunity for steady income, it's crucial to grasp the associated risks. The maximum loss is determined by the width of the spreads. To calculate the maximum loss, subtract the net credit received from the width of the spreads. For example, if the call spread has a width of $5, and the put spread has a width of $4, the total width is $9. If the net credit received is $2, the maximum loss is $7 ($9 – $2). We suggest beginning with a $1 dollar spread and then widen the spread if you can afford the maximum loss in that trade.

ADAPTABILITY AND CONTINUOUS MONITORING

Adaptability is a cornerstone of successful iron condor trading. Regularly monitor the trade and be prepared to make adjustments. If the market deviates significantly, adjustments might involve rolling the spread, changing strike prices, or even converting the iron condor into an iron butterfly to better align with evolving market conditions.

In summary, mastering the iron condor strategy involves a meticulous approach to selecting strikes, collecting premiums, and managing risks. The delicate balance between risk and reward requires continuous monitoring and, if needed, adjustments. As with any trading strategy, a solid understanding of market dynamics and a commitment to ongoing learning are integral to achieving consistent success with iron condors.

SETTING IT UP

This is what an Iron Condor looks like with our setup. In the image below, we have picked a delta around -0.16 for our first put sell and around 0.16 for the call sell. We've also added two bought options just outside for protection, forming the wings of the Iron Condor. When the price stays within the area of our trades, we will make a profit. If it moves outside, then it's time to adjust or take a loss.

The four parts of this type of setup are called the wings of the Iron Condor, as shown in the image below.

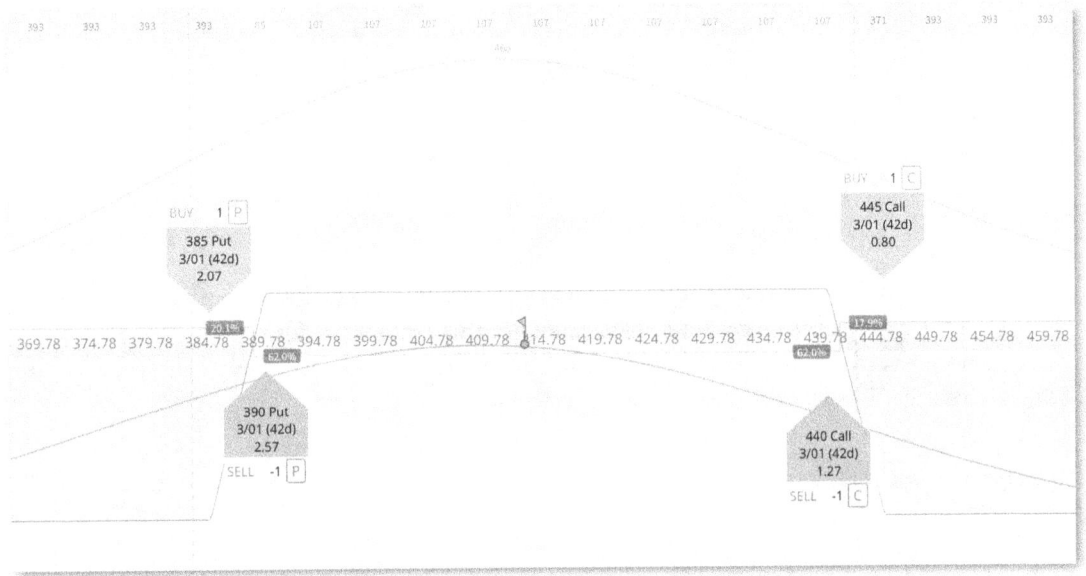

In the example above we have sold a put and a call with around 0.16 delta. Then we bought a put and a call $5 under and above the other two ones. We would like the price to stay in the middle area until expiration. We usually pick an expiration date around 45 days when we trade Iron Condors.

We like to exit the trade either when reaching a 50% or when we have 21 days until expiration.

We usually use Iron Condors on SPY, TLT, GLD, FXI, XRT, XLP, EEM, XLU, XOP, and XBI. Most of the time, we use a trading bot to find the right time for these Iron Condors. At the time this book was written, everything worked fine for us. If you like trading this way, check our website for more information. Please note that we may have made adjustments since then; therefore, we won't include exact details of our current trading approach in this book. Simply visit the following link: **tradeoptionsteam.com/bots**

We have been talking a lot about setting up alerts in some of the strategies. This is, of course, different in every broker platform. So, we are showing how to do this in the platform we use. You can probably find information on how to do this if you use another broker when trading options. Or you can ask the support people that are supposed to help you with things like that.

In one example we wanted to set an alert when a trade moves to -0.30 delta or above. We look for the price at around -0.30 delta, and in this example we end up at $4,760.

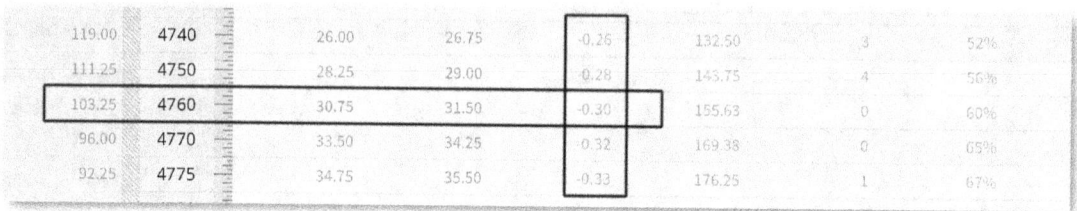

119.00	4740		26.00	26.75	-0.26	132.50	3	52%
111.25	4750		28.25	29.00	-0.28	143.75	4	56%
103.25	4760		30.75	31.50	-0.30	155.63	0	60%
96.00	4770		33.50	34.25	-0.32	169.38	0	65%
92.25	4775		34.75	35.50	-0.33	176.25	1	67%

Then we look at our tab on the right side to find the Bell symbol, which is where we set the alert. We set the price to the level we want to trigger, and in this example we also select <(less than), since we want the trigger to alert us when the price moves here or lower. You will also see a list of other active triggers below this area, if you have any active.

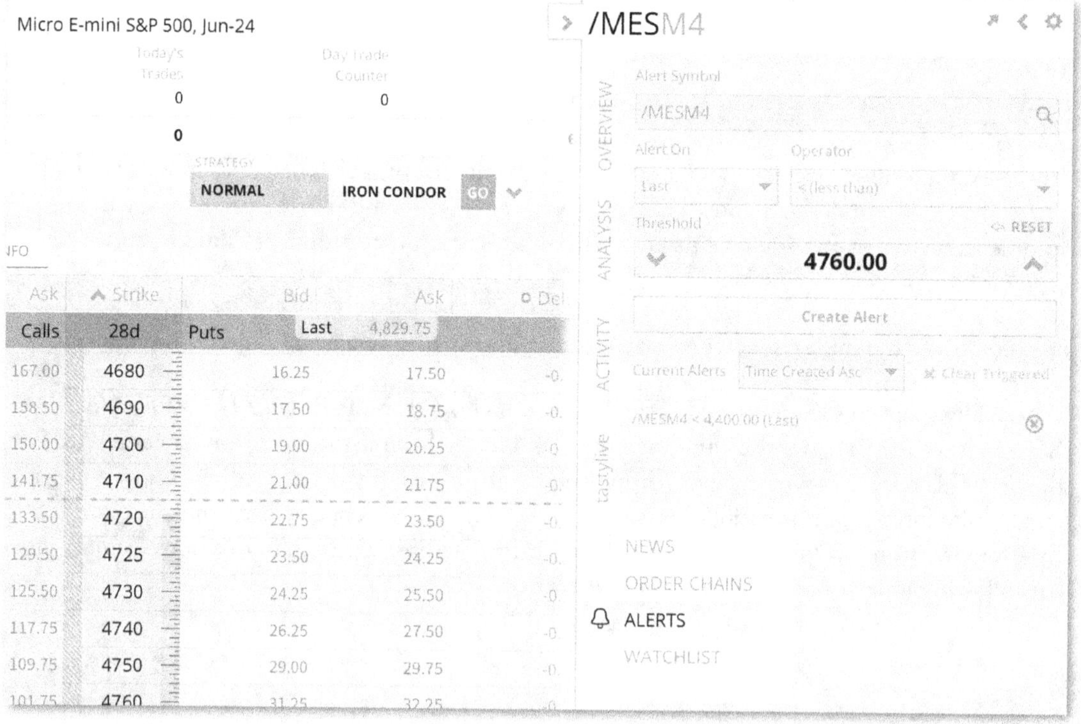

Micro E-mini S&P 500, Jun-24

> /MESM4

	Today's Trades	Day Trade Counter	
	0	0	
	0		

STRATEGY

NORMAL   IRON CONDOR   GO

Alert Symbol

/MESM4

Alert On	Operator
Last	<(less than)

Threshold   RESET

4760.00

Create Alert

Current Alerts   Time Created Asc   Clear Triggered

/MESM4 < 4,400.00 (Last)

IFO

Ask	Strike	Puts	Bid	Ask	Del
Calls	28d		Last	4,829.75	
167.00	4680		16.25	17.50	-0
158.50	4690		17.50	18.75	-0.
150.00	4700		19.00	20.25	-0
141.75	4710		21.00	21.75	-0.
133.50	4720		22.75	23.50	-0
129.50	4725		23.50	24.25	-0.
125.50	4730		24.25	25.50	-0
117.75	4740		26.25	27.50	-0
109.75	4750		29.00	29.75	-0
101.75	4760		31.25	32.25	-0

OVERVIEW ANALYSIS ACTIVITY tastylive

NEWS

ORDER CHAINS

ALERTS

WATCHLIST

The Option Greeks – Delta, Gamma, Theta, and Vega. Each Greek unravels a layer of complexity, offering a glimpse into how options dance in harmony with market movements. Here we talk about four of them. Remember, the depths of the Greeks extend far beyond these pages. You can learn a lot more about them online. We will only scratch the surface here, so you won't get bored.

THE GREEK SYMPHONY
Delta: Think of it as the heartbeat, pulsating with every movement of the underlying asset.
Gamma: This is the rhythm, anticipating changes in delta and orchestrating the future beats.
Theta: A subtle melody, marking the passage of time and its effect on option values.
Vega: The crescendo, resonating with market volatility and its impact on options.

DELTA
Delta measures how much an option's price changes for every $1 change in the underlying asset's price.
Simplified Explanation: If an option has a delta of 0.5, when the stock moves up by $1, the option price tends to increase by $0.50.

GAMMA
Gamma measures the rate of change of the option's delta concerning changes in the underlying asset's price.
Simplified Explanation: Gamma tells us how much the delta could change based on future movements in the stock price. It shows how quickly delta itself can change.

THETA
Theta measures the rate of time decay in an option's value. It indicates how much an option's value might decrease as time passes.
Simplified Explanation: Theta shows how much an option might lose in value as each day passes, especially as it gets closer to expiration. Therefore it might be a good idea to close some trades before expiration. But this is also mentioned in the strategies we discuss in this book.

VEGA
Vega measures an option's sensitivity to changes in implied volatility.
Simplified Explanation: Vega helps understand how an option's price might change when the market's expectation of future price movements (volatility) changes.

These Greeks help traders and investors understand the various factors influencing an option's price and how it might behave concerning changes in the underlying asset's price, time passing, volatility shifts, and interest rate movements.

Trading options can be thrilling, but without a clear plan, it's like setting sail without a map. A trading plan acts as your guide, helping you navigate the unpredictable seas of the market with direction and confidence.

You should treat your trading as a business. Every business have a budget, no matter if it's a small company or one like Apple or Microsoft. If you want to be profitable, you should have a plan with rules. And you should stick to that plan when you know it's working. Otherwise you will probably not be profitable.

You should write down the rules you have for your trades. What are your rules for entering and exiting a trade. When do you need to adjust your trades. What are your guidelines. Why did you adjust something. Why and when did you exit a trade.

Then it's always good to write down the date you entered and exited the trade, the strike prices you used, what strategy you employed, the profit/loss for the trade, your profit target for the trade, and your profit goal per month and per year. Is it 2% per month, 3% per month, or maybe 4% per month? When you have a trading plan with working strategies, you should follow it, be consistent, and repeat the rules you have set up. Practices like these will help you on your way to making a profit.

If you have a working trading plan, then stick to it. Don't add any new strategies. Don't change the strategies you use. Stick to your plan as long as it's doing what it's supposed to do.

If you follow a good trading plan with rules that works for you, then you don't have to sit and watch your trades all day long.

THE FOUNDATION OF YOUR PLAN

A trading plan is your personalized roadmap to success in options trading. It sets out your objectives, strategies, and guidelines for handling trades – a document essential for any trader. Whether you prefer writing it down on paper or setting up a digital spreadsheet, it's your compass through the market's twists and turns. Microsoft Word, Excel, Numbers, Google Docs, or Google Sheets are all great tools for things like this.

RECORDING YOUR TRADES

Record each trade: strategy used, days until expiry, entry/exit prices, and the money involved. Note how you felt or why you made the trade. This helps learn from wins and losses. Whether it's The Wheel Strategy, Iron Condors, or other strategies, keeping these notes shows your progress and trade patterns.

THE ART OF CONSISTENCY

Being consistent is really important. Decide when you'll start and stop a trade before you begin. If your trade needs changes, figure out what needs to happen for those adjustments. Sticking to your plan helps you avoid making decisions based on how you feel and keeps you focused on what you want to achieve.

STRATEGIES IN FOCUS
Explain your strategies well. Describe how you choose trades, decide how big they should be, and handle risks. Make clear how you make decisions and what rules you follow.

RISK MANAGEMENT: AN ESSENTIAL ELEMENT
Risk management is the guardian of your trading capital. While we will delve deeper into this later in the book, your trading plan should hint at the importance of this critical aspect. Specify how you intend to protect your capital and manage risk within your trades.

REVIEW, ADAPT, EVOLVE
Your trading plan should evolve as you do. Regularly review and adjust it based on your experiences. Learn from both successful trades and those that didn't quite go according to plan. Adaptation is the key to growth in the dynamic world of options trading.

LEARNING AND GROWTH MINDSET
Approach trading with a learning mindset. Every trade is a lesson. Embrace the learning opportunities and use your plan as a tool for continuous improvement. Flexibility and adaptability are vital for growth as a trader.

Ultimately, a trading plan isn't just about profits. It's about discipline, strategy, and a mindset geared towards continuous improvement. By adhering to your plan, you lay the groundwork for a prosperous journey in options trading.

WHAT TO USE
You can always set up a plan for when to trade the different strategies you want to trade. What strategy will you use in a bullish market, when you think the underlying is going up. What strategy to use in a bearish market, when you think the market will go down? And finally, what strategy to use in a neutral market when you think the market will move sideways and just a little up and down, or when you have no idea where the market is going.

In a bullish market, you could use something like a "Bull Call Spread".

In a neutral market you could use an "Iron Condor" or a "Strangle".

And finally, in a bearish market you might use a "Bear Call Spread".

People use technical indicators in charts to find out where the market is heading. A lot of people use the indicator Relative Strength Index (RSI) to determine the direction. Others use the Stochastic indicator in a similar way. Some use the Moving Average, and most people use a combination of different indicators, so you might want to find one setup that you like and understand. Don't use too many indicators; it's usually better to find two or three that work well together.

This chapter is super important. Many traders forget it, but successful ones always remember it – always. Imagine this: think of risk management like a shield. It keeps your trading adventure safe and going strong. Paying attention to this part can make a huge difference in how you trade.

There are so many people just looking at the profit for each trade. Try to do it the other way around. Look for the max loss in that trade. Look at the worst case scenario. Can you afford it. Maybe you are risking too much.

Don't use too much of your buying power. A good rule is to be below 50% of your available buying power.

THE ESSENTIAL 2%

Think of your trades like seeds in a garden. Spread them out. Don't risk more than 2% of all your seeds (or your trading money) in one spot. This keeps your garden growing, even if one spot doesn't work well.

CRUNCHING NUMBERS IN OPTIONS LAND

Understanding risk in options trading means knowing how much money to use for each trade. If you have $1,000 to trade with, risking only 2% means using just $20 for a trade. But the strategies we discuss might need more than $1,000. For instance, starting the Wheel strategy might need around $5,000 for better opportunities with stronger stocks.

When you have higher funds, there's more risk if you're assigned 100 stocks. Let's say a stock costs $15 each. To risk only 2%, you'd need $75,000. If you don't have that much, it's safer to start with the Wheel strategy until you have enough. If you have $1,500 in your account, you could trade Cash Secured Puts on a $15 stock or less. To run two trades like that at once, you'd need $3,000. But if you have $5,000, you could trade one stock at $30 and another at $20, or even two at $15 and one at $20, as long as you can afford to buy 100 shares if you get assigned. Just add up the total amount for all the trades you have open at the same time.

THE WHYS OF 2%

Why stick to this 2% rule? Picture the market like a rollercoaster ride – exciting but wild. Risking a small part means you can enjoy the ride without worry.

THE BRAVE 5% STEP

Some might want to risk 5%. It's like taking a big leap in an adventure. But remember, big risks mean big falls.

CONSISTENCY, THE HERO'S WAY

Successful traders are really good at being consistent. They stick to their plans, just like heroes stick to their missions. Staying consistent with your risk plan helps avoid surprises in trading.

THE FINAL WISDOM, UNVEILED

Why do people talk so much about the 2% rule? It's like a special secret – it keeps you in the trading game, even when things get tricky.

THE GREAT PROTECTOR: RISK-ADJUSTED STRATEGIES

Check out strategies that match how much risk you're okay with. Some are more adventurous, while others are steadier. Pick what fits your style.

THE TREASURE OF PATIENCE

Trading isn't a sprint. It's about growing your garden slowly and protecting it from surprises.

THE POWER OF LEARNING

Always keep learning! Every trade teaches something. Use your trading plan to learn and become a better trader. That's how you build a stronger shield for future trades.

Remember, go slow. Rushing might not end well. Stick to your plan, follow what successful traders do, and trade without emotions. Your trading adventure will surely flourish!

We're delving into the world of margin accounts in options trading in this chapter. Let's break down what it is and how it works in a straightforward manner!

In finance, we often hear about "margin," which is essentially money borrowed from a broker for buying investments. Now, let's focus on "option margin" – it's the money you set aside to cover potential losses from options contracts, like a safety deposit.

Different Margins: Options have varying margin requirements depending on the exchange. This is influenced by the investment's risk and the time left for it to expire.

More Buying Power: With option margin, you can control more stocks with less money. For instance, if you have $10,000, you can buy an options contract worth $20,000 by using $10,000 and borrowing the rest.

BENEFITS OF USING OPTION MARGIN
Option margin offers some benefits for investors.

More Buying Power: Lets you buy more stocks with less money, potentially doubling profits.

Lower Costs: Margin loans usually have lower interest rates, reducing trading costs.

Hedging: Reduces risk by using margin to buy put options, offsetting potential losses.

Diversification: Helps spread risk by investing in various securities.

Remember, while option margin has advantages, it also involves extra risk. Consider your finances, goals, and risk tolerance before using it.

RISKS OF USING OPTION MARGIN
Using option margin can be profitable, but it has risks.

Margin Calls: If your account value drops, the broker may ask for more money, potentially leading to selling assets and more losses.

Volatility Risk: Options are unpredictable, and using margin magnifies the unpredictability. Small price changes can lead to significant losses.

RISK MANAGEMENT STRATEGIES

Let's discuss what you can do to manage these risks.

Know the Risks: Understand how margin works, potential margin calls, and market changes.

Use Stop-Loss Orders: Set orders to sell an option if it reaches a certain price to limit losses. This is what we use in some of our strategies when we don't have protection or don't want to be assigned the underlying.

Avoid Over-Leveraging: Use only as much money as you can afford to lose.

Have a Solid Trading Plan: Include entry and exit points, stop-loss orders, and a maximum margin in your trading plan. We have a whole chapter about this because we think it's very important.

In conclusion, option margin can increase buying power, but understanding and managing risks is crucial.

BROKERAGE REQUIREMENTS FOR OPTION MARGIN TRADING

Option margin trading involves borrowing money from brokers to buy investments. Brokers set strict rules due to the higher risk.

Minimum Balance: Brokers may require a higher minimum balance for option margin trading, such as $10,000 or more.

Approval Process: A more detailed approval process may include additional paperwork or background checks.

Margin Maintenance: After approval, investors must maintain a minimum amount in their account. Falling below triggers a margin call.

Risks and Rewards: Option margin trading has risks and rewards. While it increases buying power, it can lead to significant losses. Research yourself, and you can always consult a financial advisor before starting.

CALCULATING MARGIN REQUIREMENTS FOR OPTIONS

Understanding margin requirements for options is crucial.

Different Options, Different Margins: Call and put options have varied margin requirements depending on the type.

Percentage of Option Value: Margin is a percentage of the option's value, based on the strike price and underlying asset's price.

Substantial Requirements: Margin requirements can be substantial. Ensure you have enough funds to cover them.

Reduce Requirements with Strategies: Options strategies like spreads can lower margin requirements.

Monitor Requirements: Keep a close eye on margin requirements as they can change based on the underlying asset's price and volatility.

In summary, understanding and calculating margin requirements for options are vital for successful trading.

COMMON MISTAKES TO AVOID WHEN USING OPTION MARGIN

Avoid these common mistakes when using option margin.

Not Understanding Margin Requirements: Lack of understanding can lead to margin calls and potential liquidation of accounts.

Ignoring Stop-Loss Orders: Set orders to sell an option if it hits a specific price to limit losses.

Over-Leveraging Accounts: Using too much margin increases the risk of significant losses.

Use option margin wisely, considering risks, understanding margin requirements, and having a solid trading plan.

ALTERNATIVES TO OPTION MARGIN FOR EXPANDING BUYING POWER

Consider these alternatives to option margin.

Portfolio Margin: Considers overall portfolio risk, potentially increasing leverage without added risk.

Cash Accounts: Buy securities with available cash, offering flexibility and lower trading costs.

Leveraged ETFs: ETFs using derivatives to provide multiplied performance, but they come with risks.

Futures Contracts: Agreements to buy or sell assets at a set price and date. Provides leverage but is complex and risky.

Remember, option margin is effective but not the only choice. Consider alternatives based on your goals and risk tolerance.

IS OPTION MARGIN RIGHT FOR YOU?

Before deciding if option margin is right for you, understand how it works. Option margin lets you increase buying power by borrowing money to buy options contracts.

Consider Your Risk Tolerance: It amplifies gains and losses, comes with interest charges, and broker requirements may change.

Evaluate Your Need for More Buying Power: Option margin is powerful but not necessary for trading options. Consider your financial situation and goals.

Option margin can be beneficial for experienced traders, but it's essential to understand and manage the associated risks responsibly.

Let's explore a hypothetical week incorporating the strategies from this book. Remember, it's crucial to adapt everything to align with your unique goals and risk tolerance.

THE WHEEL STRATEGY

For those diving into The Wheel Strategy, kick off by curating a list of stocks you'd like to own. In our broker platform you can make your own watchlist, which is great. We recommend focusing on stocks with dividends. We check our list of stocks (we have around 30–40 stocks in our list). If there's no earnings report scheduled in the next 30–45 days, we sell a cash secured put and pocket the premium. If we already own 100 stocks, we start selling covered calls. But we avoid doing this around earnings reports.

THE MONDAY STRATEGY

Each Monday, we implement The Monday Strategy on /MES. Typically, we wait one or two hours after the market opens before executing a trade.

THE 112 STRATEGY A

Midweek, on Wednesdays, we engage in The 112 Strategy A, targeting a 60-day expiration.

THE 112 STRATEGY B

As the month begins (and possibly in the third week if capital permits), we employ The 112 Strategy B with a 120-day expiration.

STRANGLE TRADES

We keep a watchful eye on assets like /ES, /MES, Gold, Copper, and Oil. We analyze charts with our preferred technical indicators. If conditions seem favorable and our account is sufficiently funded, we consider putting on a strangle trade.

DAILY CHECKS

We perform a daily check on our account. Assess whether any adjustments are needed or if it's time to conclude one of our trades. If a trade is closed, we contemplate initiating a new one with the same strategy. We record all activities in our Google Sheets spreadsheet.

AUTOMATIC CLOSURES

Certain trades auto-close when leveraging the close profit functions in our broker platform. Upon closure, an email notification from our broker arrives. We verify that everything unfolded as expected and meticulously document the details in our spreadsheet. This process is designed to be time-efficient. When trades align with our expectations, it's a rewarding experience. This is a snapshot of how a week might look like when applying the strategies featured in this book. And we hope you can find a way to use one or more of the strategies we use.

COMMON MISTAKES IN OPTIONS TRADING

Options trading can be tricky, especially for beginners. Let's look at some common mistakes and how to steer clear of them.

OVERLEVERAGING

What it is: Using too much borrowed money in the hope of amplifying profits.

Why it's a problem: Magnifies losses if the trade goes south.

How to avoid it: Start small, only use a fraction of your capital in each trade.

IGNORING THE GREEKS

What they are: Factors like Delta, Gamma, Theta, and Vega that affect option pricing.

Why it's a problem: Not understanding these can lead to unexpected outcomes.

How to avoid it: Learn the basics of the Greeks and monitor them in your trades.

FAILURE TO PLAN EXIT STRATEGIES

What it is: Not deciding when to exit a trade before entering.

Why it's a problem: Emotional decision-making and potential for greater losses.

How to avoid it: Have clear exit plans – know when to take profits and cut losses.

CHASING LOSSES

What it is: Trying to quickly recover losses through aggressive trading.

Why it's a problem: Can lead to impulsive decisions and more losses.

How to avoid it: Stick to your strategy, don't let emotions guide your actions.

Let's learn from these mistakes and trade wisely.

Now that you've grasped the basics, let's delve into more advanced strategies. Perhaps you're interested in exploring these strategies, especially if they align better with your preferred type of trading. We will provide a brief overview of how they work in the following chapters.

CALENDAR SPREADS

Using different expiration dates to capture time decay.

BUTTERFLY SPREADS

A strategy for when you expect the market to remain neutral.

RATIO SPREADS

Involving different quantities of options to effectively manage risk.

CREDIT SPREADS

Collect money upfront while controlling potential losses through simultaneous selling and buying of options. Utilize Bull Put Spreads for bullish markets and Bear Call Spreads for bearish markets.

These strategies demand a bit more understanding, so take your time to grasp the concepts. We will explain how each strategy works and offer insights into how you can apply them in your trading endeavors.

Calendar Spreads is a neat strategy that involves using options with different expiration dates to make the most of time decay. Now, let's break down what this means in simple terms.

Imagine you have a calendar. On this calendar, you have two dates – one closer and one farther away. In the world of options, we use this idea to our advantage.

Here's how it works: You choose one option with a closer expiration date, let's say 30 days from now. This is like the date that's closer on your calendar. Then, you pick another option with a farther expiration date, maybe 60 or 90 days away – the one that's farther on your calendar.

Now, why would you do this? It's all about time decay. You see, options lose value over time. The closer they get to their expiration date, the faster they lose value. It's like an ice cream cone melting in the sun – it just keeps melting.

With a Calendar Spread, you're betting on this time decay. You sell the option with the closer expiration date, thinking it will lose value faster, and you buy the one with the farther expiration date to protect yourself in case things don't go as planned.

Let's put it in simple terms: You're trying to make money from the faster melting of one ice cream cone while keeping another one safe in the shade.

Now, of course, there's more to it. You need to choose the right strike prices and understand how the market might move. But at its core, Calendar Spreads are about using time to your advantage. As a beginner, it's like playing with time to see how options change. It's a bit like predicting whether your ice cream will melt faster or slower. And just like with ice cream, the goal is to make a sweet profit!

SETTING UP A CALENDAR SPREAD WITH XYZ AS AN EXAMPLE

Buy one call or put option with a closer expiration date, say 30 days (e.g., XYZ $100). Sell the same type of option with a farther expiration date, perhaps 60 or 90 days away (e.g., XYZ $100).

Aim for a delta of around -0.3 for the option you buy with the closer expiration date. The option you sell with the farther expiration date could have a delta around -0.15.

Buying the closer expiration date option sets a neutral to slightly bullish tone. Simultaneously, selling the farther expiration date option generates income and helps manage risk.

If the stock price remains close to the strike price at the closer expiration date, you profit from the bought option. The sold option helps offset the cost and might add additional profit if the stock makes a significant move.

Keep in mind, this is just a basic example. Always analyze market conditions, choose appropriate strike prices based on your outlook, and consider the risk and reward. Adjust the strategy based on your preferences and market expectations.

Butterfly Spreads are like catching a gentle wave in the ocean of trading. This strategy is for times when you expect the market to remain calm and not swing too much in any direction.

Imagine you're in a boat, and the water is mostly still. You expect it to stay that way for a while. That's when you might consider using Butterfly Spreads.

Here's how it works: You pick three different options, like three points on the water. One option is like the center of your wave, and the other two are like the gentle slopes on each side.

The goal? To make money when the market stays close to that central point, just like riding a calm wave. You're not looking for big waves or storms; you're enjoying the smooth and steady movement.

Now, why would you do this? It's all about predicting the market's mood. Butterfly Spreads are for when you think the market will be neither too bullish nor too bearish, just cruising in the middle.

In simple terms, it's like betting that your boat will stay in the calm part of the ocean. You're not chasing after big waves; you're savoring the tranquility.

HOW TO SET UP BUTTERFLY SPREADS

Choose three different strike prices: Buy one call option with a lower strike (let's say XYZ $95), sell two call options with a middle strike (XYZ $100), and buy one call option with a higher strike (XYZ $105).

Position the trades: Buying the lower and higher strikes sets the neutral tone, while selling the middle strikes generates income and helps manage risk.

Understand the outcome: If the stock price remains close to the middle strike at expiration, you profit from the sold call options. The bought call options limit potential losses, making it a strategy for a stable market.

Remember, this is a basic example. Evaluate market conditions, choose appropriate strike prices, and consider the risk and reward. Adjust the strategy based on your market outlook and preferences. Then, you're ready to ride those gentle waves and navigate the tranquil waters of trading!

Ratio Spreads is like finding the right mix of ingredients for your trading recipe. It involves using different quantities of options to create a balance and manage risk effectively.

Imagine you're in a kitchen, and you're cooking up a dish. Some ingredients are essential, while others are there to add flavor. Ratio Spreads work in a similar way.

Here's how it works: Instead of using an equal amount of options, you use different quantities. It's like adjusting the proportions of salt and pepper in your recipe. You might use more of one and less of the other to get the taste just right.

The goal? To create a situation where you can benefit more if the market moves in a certain direction. It's a bit like tweaking your recipe to make it more appealing.

Now, why would you do this? It's all about finding the right balance. If you think the market might move in a particular way, you adjust your options to make the most of that movement.

In simple terms, it's like saying, "I want my trading dish to have a unique flavor, and I'll adjust the ingredients to make it perfect."

Of course, there's more to it. You need to choose the right quantities and understand how the market might move. But at its core, Ratio Spreads are about fine-tuning your options mix.

As a beginner, it's like saying, "I don't want all my ingredients to be equal; I want to play with the proportions to get the best result." Ratio Spreads are your way of creating a balanced and flavorful trading experience.

RATIO SPREAD EXAMPLE USING PUTS FOR COMPANY XYZ

Choose two strike prices: Buy one put with a lower strike (e.g., XYZ $100) and sell two puts with a slightly higher strike (e.g., XYZ $105).

Consider using delta as a guide: Buy the lower-strike put with a delta around -0.3, and sell the higher-strike puts with a delta around -0.15 each.

Position the trades: Buy the lower strike put to take a bullish position. Simultaneously, sell the two higher-strike puts to generate income and manage risk.

Understand the outcome: If the stock price remains above the lower strike at expiration, you profit from the bought put. The sold puts help offset the cost and may add additional profit if the stock rises.

Remember, this is a basic example. Evaluate market conditions and choose appropriate strike prices based on your outlook. Always consider the risk and reward when setting up any options strategy. You can also apply the same principle using calls if you anticipate a different market direction.

Credit Spreads is a clever options strategy where you sell one option and buy another at the same time. It's like putting money in your pocket upfront while also setting limits on potential losses. This approach comes in two flavors – Bull Put Spreads for when you feel the market is going up, and Bear Call Spreads for when you expect it to move down.

Imagine you're making a deal. You promise to sell something at a certain price, but at the same time, you protect yourself by buying something a bit more expensive. It's similar to selling lemonade at your stand, ensuring you won't run out by buying extra lemons.

EXAMPLE USING PUTS FOR COMPANY XYZ

Let's say XYZ is trading at around $120. For the put you sell, aim for a delta around -0.3. It's like checking the weather to make sure it's a good day for your lemonade stand. This might be around $110 where you sell the first one. Then you buy one with a slightly lower price at around $105 to make the bull credit spread.

When you sell the lower-strike put, you pocket some money upfront. This is your way of making sure you have something to show for your lemonade sales.

Understanding the outcome is always important. If the stock price stays above the lower strike at expiration, you keep the money you earned upfront. The higher-strike put acts like an umbrella, protecting you from potential losses if things don't go exactly as planned.

Remember, this is a basic example. Before setting up any strategy, consider the current market conditions, pick the right prices based on your outlook, and always think about the risks and rewards. The same idea can be applied using calls if you think the market is headed in the opposite direction.

If you believe the market is heading in the other direction, then you would take the opposite approach. You'd sell a call with a higher strike price than the current spot price and buy another call with a slightly higher strike price. This is a strategy you might employ if you anticipate the price for XYZ might go down. So, there are two ways to set up a credit spread like this: the first one if you think the market is going up, and the second one if you think the price will go down.

Analyzing the market is a crucial skill in options trading, especially for beginners. Let's delve deeper into each of the market analysis techniques to provide you with a more comprehensive understanding.

TECHNICAL ANALYSIS

Technical analysis involves studying charts, trends, and various indicators to make predictions about future price movements. Charts visually represent historical price data, helping traders identify patterns and trends. Technical indicators, such as moving averages and relative strength index (RSI), offer additional insights into potential market directions. For beginners, it's essential to explore and familiarize yourself with these charts and indicators to enhance your ability to forecast market movements.

FUNDAMENTAL ANALYSIS

Fundamental analysis considers the underlying factors that may influence an asset's value. For options trading, this involves examining earnings reports, economic indicators, and relevant news events. Earnings reports, released by companies regularly, provide insights into financial performance. Economic indicators, such as employment reports or inflation rates, can impact overall market sentiment. Staying informed about significant news events is crucial for understanding how they might affect the options market. Beginners should gradually integrate fundamental analysis into their decision-making process to gain a holistic view of potential market changes.

VOLATILITY ANALYSIS

Volatility, or the degree of price fluctuation, significantly impacts options pricing. High volatility often leads to increased option premiums, while low volatility results in lower premiums. As a beginner, understanding volatility and its effects on options is vital. The volatility index (VIX) is a common measure that reflects market expectations for future volatility. Learning to interpret the VIX and other volatility indicators can assist you in making more informed decisions about when to enter or exit options trades.

COMBINING ANALYSES

A well-rounded approach often involves combining technical, fundamental, and volatility analyses. While technical analysis helps with timing entry and exit points, fundamental analysis provides insights into the broader market context. Considering volatility adds another layer, helping you assess the potential risks and rewards of a particular options trade. As a beginner, experimenting with a blend of these analyses in your decision-making process will contribute to more comprehensive and informed trading strategies.

In essence, delving into market analysis techniques equips beginners with valuable tools to navigate the dynamic world of options trading. The key is to progressively integrate these techniques into your trading routine, gaining confidence and enhancing your ability to make strategic decisions.

Technical indicators are a powerful tool for understanding market trends and making trading decisions. In this chapter, we'll explore what technical indicators are, why they matter, and how to use them in your trading.

Technical indicators are visual representations of price movements and market behaviors. They help traders analyze historical price data and identify potential future trends. Think of them as your trading compass, guiding you through the complex terrain of the financial markets.

The financial markets are dynamic and influenced by various factors. Technical indicators provide traders with valuable insights into market trends, momentum, volatility, and potential reversals. By understanding these indicators, you can make more informed decisions about when to enter or exit a trade.

We'll show you what they look like and how to use them in your trading. There is a lot of information in books and on the internet about different indicators and how to use them. But try to find just a couple that work for you. Don't overdo it. Avoid filling your chart with too many indicators; they might get in your way. Some people just look at the charts and how the price moves, they don't even use the indicators.

We will start with Candlestick Charts, which is the one a lot of traders use when looking at a chart. Candlestick Charts are composed of a body, which can be filled or open, depending on your settings (or the default ones in the chart you are using). Then there is a whick on top and a whick at the bottom.

You can decide to look at a chart in different time frames. If you look at a chart with an hourly view, then every candle on the chart represents 1 hour. If you decide to use a daily chart, then every candle represents one day.

In the chart below, set to a daily timeframe, each candle represents one day. In this example, we can see the last 40 days, as there are 40 candles displayed.

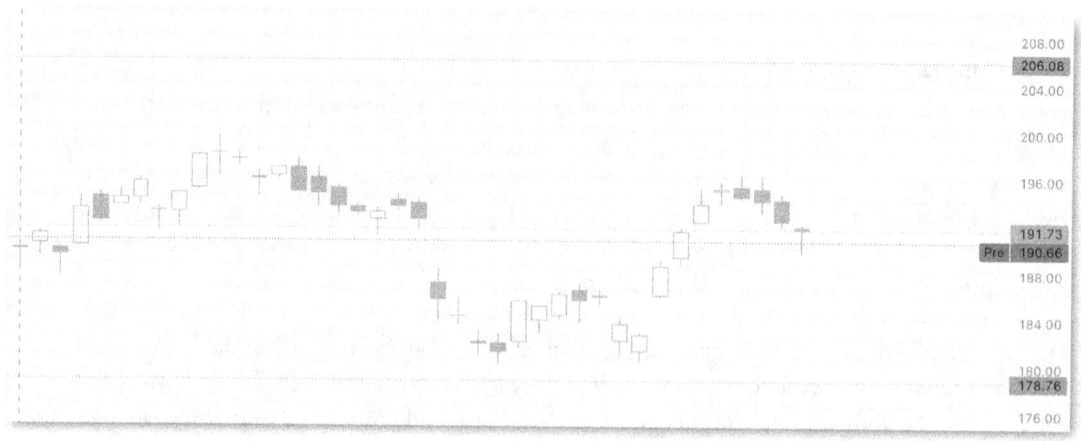

The different parts of this candle give us information about the price. If we look at the image below, there is one open candle on the left and one filled candle on the right.

If we observe this candle on an hourly chart, then a candle like this represents one hour. When the hour starts, the candle begins building from the OPEN PRICE part of the candle. During this hour, the price will move up and down, just like stock prices do all the time.

The HIGH PRICE in this image is the highest level that the price reached during that hour. The LOW PRICE is the lowest price the price moved to. Those thin lines are usually referred to as the "wick" or the "shadow" of the candle.

When we reach the last second of the hour, the price ends up at the CLOSE PRICE level that we see.

After one hour, we can see where the price was during that hour, including the highest and lowest points, as well as the starting and closing price during the hour.

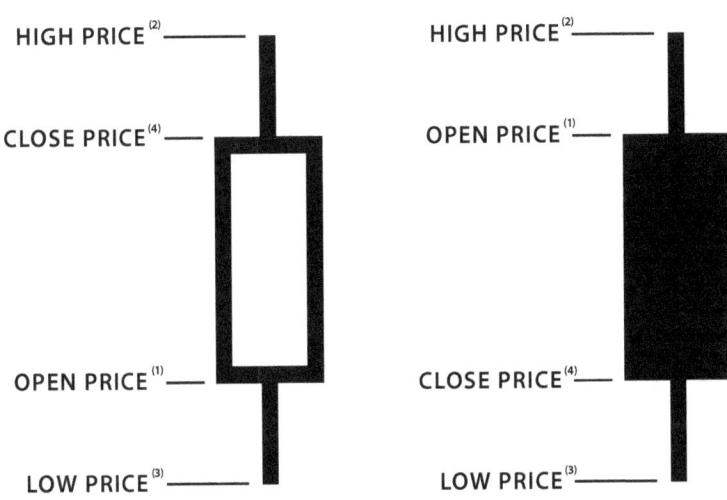

If the price was going up during this hour, we would have the open price lower, as seen in the left image. The price opened in the lower wide part, and after one hour, it closed at the upper wide part.

Then a new candle would start building next to that one on the chart. If the price was going down during the next hour, it would look something like the right image, where the candle is building from the "open price" part, and it would close below that price, shown in the lower wide part of the image, indicating that the price was going down during this hour.

Some people use green color for the candlesticks going up and red color for those going down, which is also easier to spot when you look at a lot of candles on a chart.

You can see open and filled candles in the image on the previous page, where the price has moved up and down during 40 days, as every candle in that image represents one day. You can see that every candle looks different, as the price moved up and down, reaching different high and low levels during those days.

The easiest way to learn how a candlestick builds up, is to watch a chart with a minute time frame. Then every candle represents one minute, and you will see the candles building during every minute. It is probably the easiest way to see how the candles are built while price is moving.

TECHNICAL INDICATORS FOR BEGINNERS

Relative Strength Index (RSI): RSI helps measure the speed and change of price movements. It ranges from 0 to 100, usually with readings above 70 indicating overbought conditions and readings below 30 suggesting oversold conditions.

The RSI is typically displayed below the chart, with other indicators in the main window.

In the image below you can see what the RSI look like. In this example the RSI value is 74.77, which is indicating overbought, since it is above 70. Maybe it's time for the stock to move down in a near future.

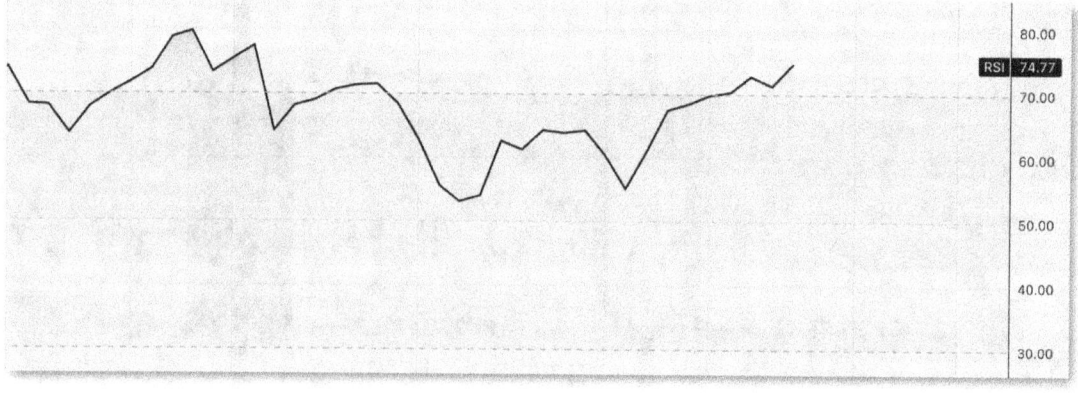

Moving Averages: Moving averages smooth out price data to create a single flowing line, making it easier to identify trends. The two main types are simple moving averages (SMA) and exponential moving averages (EMA). Moving averages smooth out the ups and downs of a stock's price over time. Let's say you're using a simple moving average over 50 days. This means each day, you take the average of the stock's prices over the past 50 days.

If the current price is above this moving average, it might suggest an upward trend. Traders sometimes use this as a signal to consider bullish options strategies. If the current price is below the moving average, it could indicate a downward trend. Traders might take this as a signal to explore bearish options strategies.

In simple terms, moving averages help traders get a smoother picture of the market's direction. If the current market price is consistently above the moving average, traders might consider bullish strategies. On the other hand, if it's consistently below, bearish strategies could be more appealing.

People use these with different settings and usually two or three of those in combination. Some like to use the 200 or 250 setting together with the 50 and the 21. And some people like to trade when two of those are crossing each other to indicate that the market is changing direction or the market is stronger in one direction. Some traders also look at the slope of the lines.

In the following image, we are looking at a daily chart, where every candlestick represents one day. The thin line below is a Moving Average with the length set to 50. The thicker line below is set to 200. This chart shows us an upward trend, as the candlesticks are above the two moving average lines.

But this is based on historical data, since the moving average is looking back to find an average of whatever length you use in the settings.

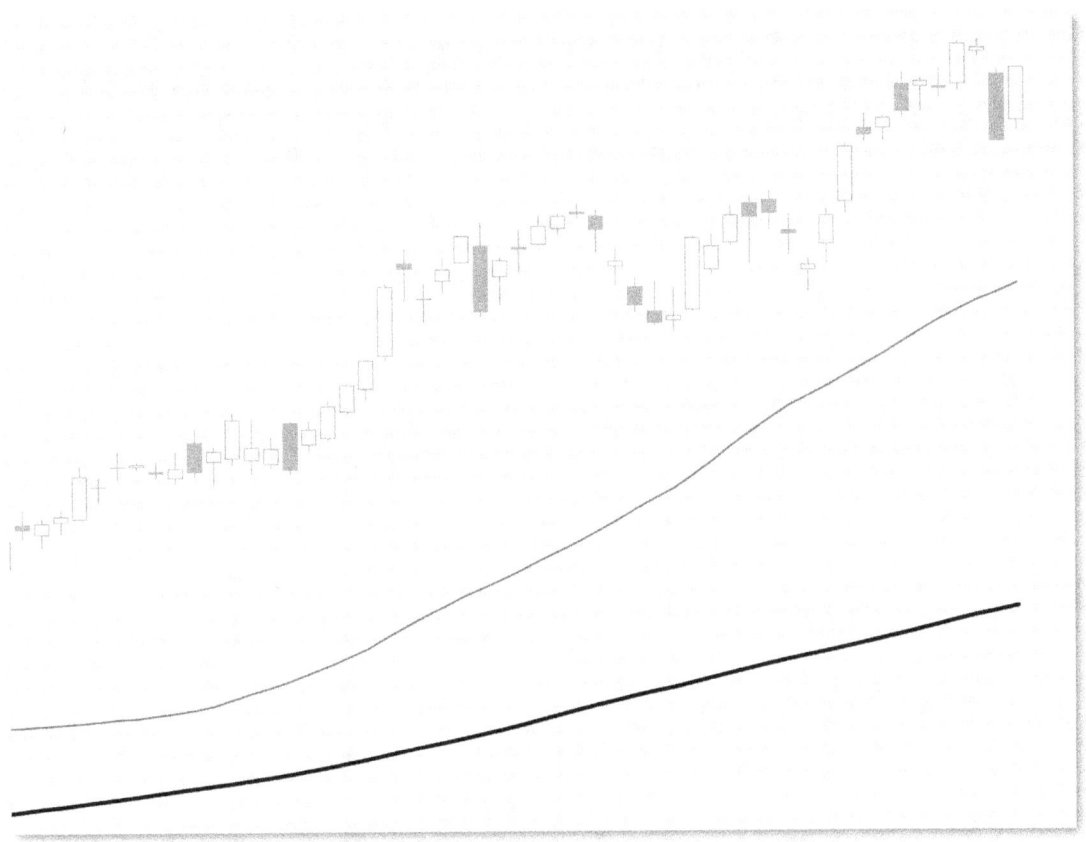

MACD (Moving Average Convergence Divergence): MACD is like a detective for trends in the stock market. It looks at how fast prices are changing by comparing two different ways of smoothing them out. When it senses a change in the air, it might signal that a new trend is about to begin. It's like having a weather forecast for the stock market!

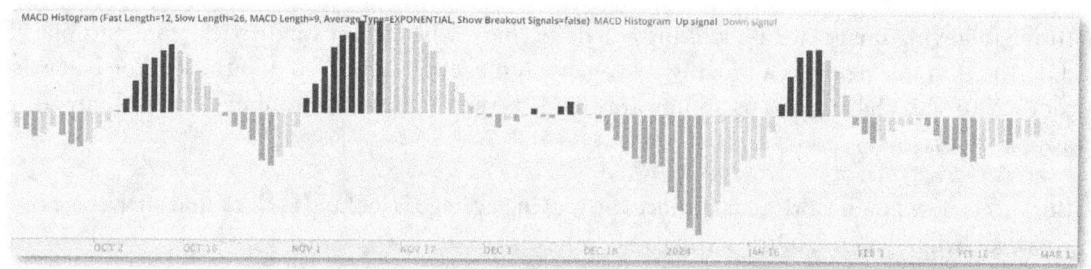

Bollinger Bands: Imagine Bollinger Bands as a tool that helps you see if a stock is relaxed or a bit excited. It has three lines – one in the middle (average), one above (a bit high), and one below (a bit low). When these lines spread out, it's like the stock is stretching, and that might mean interesting times. If they're close, it's like the stock is chilling. So, it's like a gauge, showing when the stock is in a calm zone or when it's making bigger moves.

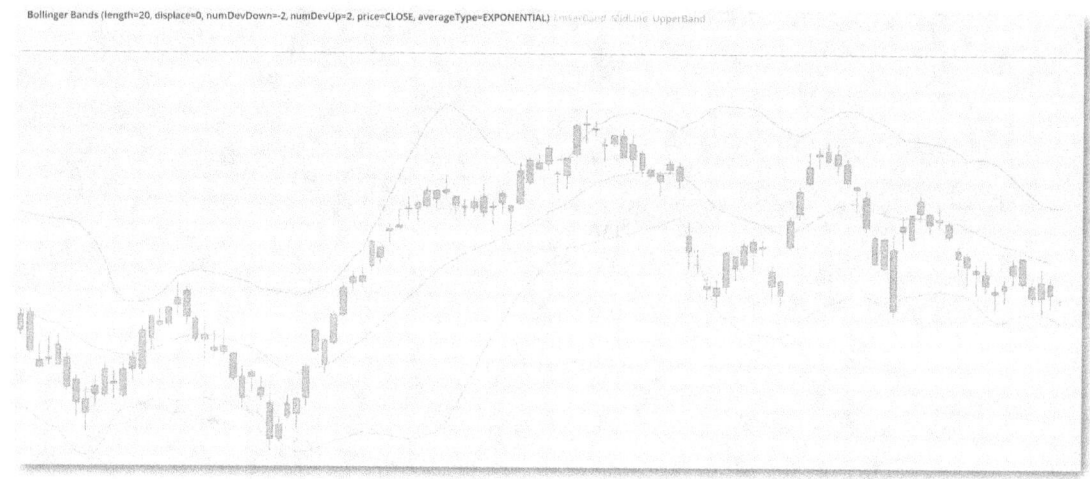

3ATR (Three Times Average True Range): Think of 3ATR as a guard keeping an eye on how wild or calm the stock market is. It considers the average true range (ATR) but triples it. ATR looks at how much a stock typically moves, and 3ATR magnifies that to see if things are extra busy or relatively quiet. If 3ATR shows a big number, it's like the market is on high alert, potentially signaling significant movements. On the other hand, a small number suggests a more relaxed market atmosphere. So, it acts as a gauge, helping you assess whether the stock is in an intense or calm phase.

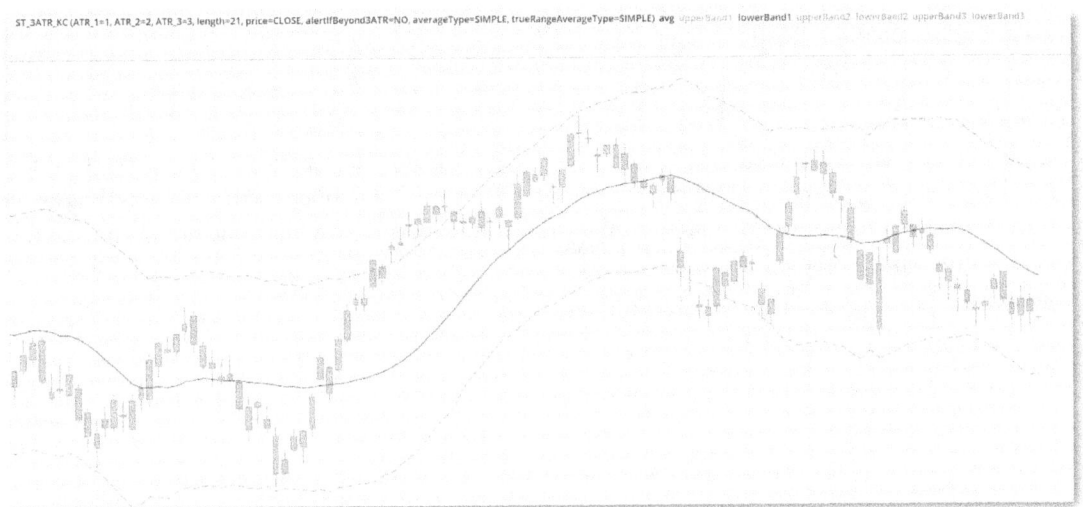

Bollinger Bands and 3ATR may seem similar at first glance, both utilizing three lines to assess market conditions, but they serve distinct purposes.

Bollinger Bands, akin to a mood gauge, measure the stock's excitement level. The three lines – upper (a bit high), middle (average), and lower (a bit low) - stretch or contract based on market movements. This tool signals whether the stock is in a calm state or making more significant moves.

On the other hand, 3ATR acts as a guard, observing how wild or calm the market is by tripling the average true range (ATR). It magnifies the typical stock movement to gauge market intensity. A large 3ATR suggests a heightened state, indicating potentially significant movements, while a smaller number indicates a more relaxed market.

In essence, while Bollinger Bands indicate the stock's emotional state, 3ATR focuses on the magnitude of market movements, providing traders with different perspectives for informed decision-making.

HOW TO USE TECHNICAL INDICATORS

Trend Identification: Use indicators to identify the direction of the prevailing trend. For example, a rising moving average suggests an uptrend.

Momentum Analysis: Gauge the strength of a price movement using indicators like RSI or MACD. Strong momentum can indicate a robust trend.

Confirmation of Patterns: Technical indicators can confirm chart patterns, providing additional validation for potential trades.

CONCLUSION

As a beginner, technical indicators can seem overwhelming at first, but with practice, you'll gain confidence in using them to enhance your trading strategies. Remember, technical analysis is an art that combines science and intuition. Take your time, experiment with different indicators, and gradually incorporate them into your trading routine. Before you know it, you'll be navigating the markets with newfound clarity and precision.

Navigating the realm of options trading involves more than just crunching numbers; it requires a profound understanding of the psychological aspects that shape successful trading strategies. Let's explore in greater detail the psychological elements that can impact your journey in options trading.

UNDERSTANDING EMOTIONS

Emotions play a crucial role in trading. Fear, greed, and overconfidence are common emotions that can influence decision-making. Being aware of these emotional triggers is the first step towards maintaining a balanced approach. Recognizing when fear might drive you to exit a trade prematurely or when greed may push you to overcommit is crucial. By acknowledging these emotions, you empower yourself to make more rational and informed choices.

DISCIPLINE AND PATIENCE

Discipline and patience are the cornerstones of successful trading. Crafting a well-thought-out trading plan is one thing; adhering to it with discipline is another. Patience is the antidote to impulsiveness. Not every trade will result in a win, and that's okay. Sticking to your trading strategy, even when tempted to make changes, is vital for success.

COPING WITH LOSSES

Losing is normal in trading. Instead of seeing it as a problem, think of losses as helpful lessons. Understanding what went wrong is important for getting better. Take the chance to figure out what adjustments you need, and keep going. Don't get down about it; every loss is a step toward becoming a more experienced trader.

VISUALIZATION TECHNIQUES

The power of visualization in trading should not be underestimated. Before executing a trade, take a moment to visualize its success. Picture how your well-thought-out plan unfolds positively. Visualization helps anchor your focus and keeps emotions in check. By mentally preparing for various scenarios, you equip yourself to handle unexpected market movements with composure.

Trading extends beyond the charts and graphs; it's about mastering the intricate landscape of your own mind. Discipline and focus are your allies in this venture. Discipline safeguards you from impulsive decisions, while focus ensures that emotions don't overshadow your strategic approach. As you navigate the exciting world of options trading, remember that understanding and managing your own psychology is an invaluable skill that can elevate your trading game to new heights. Stay disciplined, stay focused, and embrace the psychological journey alongside the numerical complexities of options trading.

In the world of options trading, having the right stuff is super important. Let's break down each part to help you on your trading journey.

BOOKS – GET THE KNOWLEDGE

Start by reading books that teach you the basics and some fancier stuff too. They cover all sorts of things, from beginner strategies to advanced tricks, and even how to manage risks and analyze markets.

COURSES AND WEBINARS – LEARN ONLINE

Take classes online that are made for beginners. They're full of tips from traders who've been around. Also, don't forget about webinars. These are like online seminars where experts share real-time tips.

TRADING SOFTWARE – USE THE RIGHT TOOLS

Get yourself some reliable trading software. These tools help you look at charts, screen options, and analyze stuff. Tastyworks, and TradingView are examples of good platforms. They make it easy to see what's happening in the market and help you make smart decisions.

FINANCIAL NEWS – STAY IN THE LOOP

Keep up with the latest news about money. Websites like Bloomberg, CNBC, and Investopedia share what's happening in real-time. They give you info, analyses, and expert opinions. Staying connected to these sources helps you understand the money world better.

TRADING COMMUNITIES – CONNECT WITH OTHERS

Join online groups where traders like you hang out. Platforms like Discord, Reddit's options trading group or StockTwits are good places to chat, share tips, and learn from others. Being part of these groups expands your trading circle and lets you see different ways people trade.

These things together make a cool toolkit for figuring out options trading. Dive into these opportunities, and may your trading journey be full of smart moves and successful trades.

Just as you spread investments across various stocks (if you are a stock investor), consider diversifying your options trading strategies too. Don't rely on a single approach; write down how many trades you'd like with strategies such as The Wheel or Iron Condors each month.

Some traders skip individual stocks, focusing solely on options like the 112 or strangles, often on assets like Spy, Gold, or Copper. This minimizes risk compared to depending on the fate of individual stocks.

Select what suits you best. Don't blindly follow others; find strategies that align with your style. This book introduces diverse trading strategies to help you discover what works for you.

Keep in mind, we're not experts, and this book doesn't provide financial advice. It shares our experiences and strategies we have found online that we like. Follow a plan that fits your needs and keep learning. Ignore promises of quick riches. Slow and steady growth, like aiming for 3% monthly, is more achievable.

Options Trading has much to explore. Take your time, understand the basics, and delve into new terms. We hope this book has given you a good start.

Best of luck on your trading journey, and remember – don't put all your eggs in one basket!

Good Luck

RYAN – FRED – STEVE – CAROLINE

If you found value in this book, please consider leaving a review on Amazon (use the qr code below). Your feedback is incredibly important and helps others discover the insights shared here. Wishing you success and happy trading!

tradeoptionsteam.com